THE TRUE SUBJECT

Writers on Life and Craft

EDITED BY KURT BROWN

GRAYWOLF PRESS

SAINT PAUL

Royalties for this publication accrue to the benefit of Writers' Conferences
and Festivals, a national organization of conference directors.

Acknowledgments

"Doing Good Work Together" by William Kittredge, and "Hearing Silence:
Western Myth Reconsidered," by Marilynne Robinson first appeared in
Northern Lights, Volume VIII, Number 2, 1992.

"The True Subject: The Poetry of Faiz Ahmed Faiz" by Agha Shahid Ali
first appeared in *Grand Street*, Vol. 9, #2, 1990.

"Auden's Generalizations" by Sydney Burris first appeared in
Shenandoah, Summer 1993.

Publication of this volume is made possible in part by a grant provided by
the Minnesota State Arts Board through an appropriation by the Minnesota State
Legislature, and by a grant from the National Endowment for the Arts.
Additional support has been provided by the Jerome Foundation, the Mellon
Foundation, the Lila Wallace–Reader's Digest Fund, and other generous
contributions from foundations, corporations, and individuals. Graywolf Press
is a member agency of United Arts, Saint Paul. To these organizations
and individuals who make our work possible,
we offer heartfelt thanks.

Published by GRAYWOLF PRESS
2402 University Avenue
Saint Paul, Minnesota 55114.
All rights reserved.

9 8 7 6 5 4 3 2
First Printing, 1993

Library of Congress Cataloging-in-Publication Data
The True subject : writers on life and craft / edited by Kurt Brown ;
[essays by Jane Smiley . . . et al.].
p. cm.
ISBN 1-55597-181-4 (pbk.)
1. Authorship. 2. Literature–Philosophy. I. Brown, Kurt.
II. Smiley, Jane.
PN151.T74 1993
808'.02 – dc20 92-43508

Printed in the United States of America.

CONTENTS

This volume is dedicated to the good people who organize writers' conferences, providing a forum for discussion of the True Subject, and to writers, whose bravery in conquering the blank page, and in allowing their work and lives to be judged by others, is heartily applauded.

PREFACE

Every year, in a type of seasonal migration, writers emerge from their customary isolation to gather at hundreds of small and large conferences across the United States and abroad. They meet to learn from each other, share secrets of technique and craft, and discuss methods of economic survival.

At almost all of these programs, besides teaching and reading their work aloud, established writers deliver lectures that testify to the lessons they have learned. Some of these lectures are informal, some quite polished; many are aimed directly at practicing writers, illuminating aspects of technique and craft; still others focus on topics of interest primarily to scholars.

Now and then one hears talks of a more general nature, talks that have something profound and remarkable to say about how all of us live our lives. These lectures, especially, deserve a much wider audience than the fifty to one hundred conference participants who hear them. *The True Subject* is the first of a series of annual anthologies celebrating the solid contribution writers make to our knowledge of ourselves and the world we share. A number of directors of writers' conferences helped select outstanding recent lectures and essays for this anthology.

Poems, novels, and fine essays are not rarified things, separate from our society, but, at their best, issue directly from its heart and soul. The finest writers are some of the finest contemporary philosophers – not academic philosophers of Being, but rather philosophers of the common life. They are profoundly engaged in the concerns of their time, individually and *particularly*, and have taken the opportunity a lecture affords to think deeply about what matters to them most. Motherhood. The land. Nature. Community. Failure. Success. Children. Persistence. Political responsibility. Whether or not we can ever hope that people will listen to us. The important things. The true subject.

Proceeds from this volume are donated to a new international association of writers' conferences, workshops, and festivals – people and organizations that provide writers and thinkers with a place to exchange ideas, and with the space and time to write about them.

Kurt Brown
Executive Director, *Writers' Conferences and Festivals*
December 1992

JANE SMILEY

Can Mothers Think?

[ASPEN WRITERS' CONFERENCE]

The first summer I taught at Iowa State, my 8:30 class was across the campus from my office, and I walked there briskly every day, across the grass, through the trees, and over the fences, rather than along the walks. I was seven months pregnant, thirty-three years old, and I needed to feel that this wasn't the end of my tomboy youth. I taught modern fiction, including five days of Kafka – "A Hunger Artist," "The Metamorphosis," "A Country Doctor," "In the Penal Colony." I wanted to imbue my fourteen undergraduate students with the enthusiasm for Kafka's work that I had, for its richness of meaning, its mysteriousness, its elusiveness. I remember, though, that it struck me one day as I was climbing one of those fences that it was very strange to be teaching Kafka and to be pregnant at the same time, pregnant by choice. My first thought, one of those superstitions of pregnancy on the order of rabbits and harelips, was that the child would be affected. I managed to set that one aside.

But I did not manage to resolve the uneasiness I felt at suddenly finding myself to be a living paradox, simultaneously carrying and professing hope and despair, in my head a devoted modernist, in my body a traditionalist of the most basic kind. Such a thing seemed clownish at least, and maybe impossible at worst.

And, since the early seventies, feminist literary historians had been exploring the lives of women writers, seeking to understand the relationship between pen and gender, between literary production and human reproduction. This relationship has generally been found to be a hostile one, and the hostilities have been traced to many sources, including but not limited to notions of the pen as "a metaphorical penis"; creation as "an act of Godlike solitude and pride"; the triviality of traditional women's education; feminine habits of submissiveness, modesty, and selflessness; female anxiety about authorship; and of course the demands of family, domestic, and social life. As a young writer, I wasn't aware of *all* the obstacles in my path, but I didn't need scholars to tell me the basic and irreducible fact that all the authors I had spent my life admiring and emulating – Eliot, Woolf, Austen, the Brontës, Emily Dickinson – were childless, if not, indeed, also without husbands and lovers. The writers I knew of with children wrote books like *Please Don't Eat the Daisies*. The acme of *motherly* wisdom seemed to be Erma Bombeck. Even so, my goal since college has been to become not a popular humorist but a novelist of "grace, power, and wisdom."

When I first started writing, I avidly looked for signs and portents of the future. This went beyond astrology, beyond staring at my palm trying to decide if my "fame" line was actually well defined or not. If I want to recapture what raw ambition felt like, I remember how I used to read biographies of authors as possible maps for my own life. I read them with fear and longing. Those lives didn't seem very happy, very enlarged by art, very well integrated or even, for that matter, very much fun. Clearly the wages of modernism. And I was a devoted modernist. I knew that the path to great artistry was as well defined in these biographies as the concrete walks between the buildings at Iowa State. The monuments of modernism and postmodernism distributed along the path were easy to see. There were writers then who frightened me, who liked to say, you'll never be a writer if you (fill in the blank) or if you don't (fill in the blank). I listened to them as avidly as I inspected that fame line or read those biographies.

Okay. I chose to be a writer. I had chosen to have one child. So far, so good. Alice Walker had chosen to have one child. She defended her choice in *Ms.* magazine. But, as far as I knew, she had not chosen to have a family of children, and here I was pregnant a second time, dividing myself even more deeply from the main body of admirable women writers. And here, in the summer of 1982, was Kafka. "In the Penal Colony," eerily prefiguring the Holocaust, was about torture. "A Hunger Artist" was about chronic failure to find satisfaction in the world. "The Metamorphosis" was about the experience of the self as an insect. And behind these were the other readings in the course, none of them hopeful about parent-child relations – *Native Son, To the Lighthouse, The Man Who Loved*

Children, Seize the Day. Once I had read and understood and loved them, once I had *bought* what they had to say, could I repudiate them for *Please Don't Eat the Daisies* just because I was pregnant? That seemed a lot like a deathbed conversion to me, panicky and intellectually dishonorable. On the other hand, could I read them aloud to my children, bedtime stories about how real, serious, thinking people saw the world I was bringing them into?

Does such uneasiness engage a woman writer more than it does a man? To answer this question, I polled two of my colleagues at Iowa State, Joe Geha, whose collection *Through and Through* was published in 1990 by Graywolf Press, and Steve Pett, whose novel, *Sirens*, appeared in 1990 from Vintage. Their answers were more interesting than I had expected them to be. Yes, each of them said, he had felt a strong contradiction between aspirations of literary greatness and having children. Both felt uneasy about introducing a child to the modern, and modernist, world that we live in. Joe, however, found himself letting go of this contradiction when his wife became pregnant with his first child. He had lost control over the issue – the die was cast and real life, you might say, resolved things. Steve, too, strongly felt the contradiction, and still feels it, in spite of the existence of two sons, eleven years old and five years old. The contradiction is resolved, but not dissolved – Steve feels divided both spiritually (by a necessary optimism) and practically (by a choice to live a stable middle-class life) from a place where (I couldn't quite pin him down on this) a somehow greater, wilder, or freer art has its sources. Let's call that the Romantic position. Polling my colleagues was illuminating for me, because I had assumed this to be a female question. I see that alongside the female question is a more general one that has to do, perhaps, with the conjunction of seeing and choice. Every writer, man and woman, seeks to see truly. The true modernist or postmodernist vision is a vision of disintegration, disorientation, anxiety, anomie. And reproduction, since the invention of the birth control pill, is no longer visited upon one. It is a choice that all writers feel the weight of, male or female.

And yet what my colleagues had to say also highlighted for me the characteristically female question. On the one hand, I never felt, as Joe did, that once I was pregnant, the die was cast, or that the issue was out of my control. It seemed more tenuous than that for me. Along with and

part of the fact of carrying the baby was the knowledge that the pregnancy could fail or could be brought to an untimely end. The pregnancy
was not a choice made and done with, but an assertion of choice that got
bulkier and more certain every day, but would not actually have being in
the world until the crisis of birth had been successfully weathered. But
this leaves the issue of middle-class domestic life. If I did not find it especially confining, was that because I was too dull to sense a place somewhere else, where a freer and wilder and truer art could have its sources
for me? I was looking for signs, paths and portents.

No denying it, our literary culture is built upon the works of many
women and a number of men (Kafka, Keats, Wordsworth, Whitman)
who did not have children. One effect of this is clearly the notion that
Steve Pett shares, that life without children provides a freer, and perhaps
more disinterested, vantage point for passionate observation, that parents must be so whittled away by mundane, piecemeal concerns that a
larger artistic vision is necessarily destroyed, or at least lost sight of. Steve
said to me, "I don't think about larger existential questions as much anymore. Some days it's all I can do to figure out how to get everyone home
at five o'clock." This wilder, freer art claims for itself a broader, more disinterested, and therefore truer truth. This is often accompanied by dis-
dain for the middle class, for the safety and security that the middle class
seems to seek, largely as a response to the perceived needs of children for
safety, routine, stability, order, and the daily felt love of their parents.
Ernest Hemingway's intense hostility toward Oak Park, Illinois, comes
to mind, as does nearly everything Henry Miller wrote and stood for. Arguments with middle-class life are a convention of American literature.

But we can argue about the mix of fathers and nonfathers in our literary
culture. More crucial, and perhaps less coincidental, it seems to me, is
the extreme paucity of mothers, and of the tradition of a maternal vision.
What do we know about mothers from reading our literature? We know
two things only, it seems to me. We know what they look like and we
know what others feel about them. The figure of the mother, seen from
the child's point of view, is a common one in literature, but its familiarity
doesn't make it less mysterious or illusory, since every child's view of his
or her mother is compounded of so many wishes and needs and resentments and fears, not to mention pre-verbal imprintings, that the child's
view *must* be unreliable. And then there are depictions of the mothers of

one's children. Feminist literary scholarship has done an excellent job, in the last twenty years, of pointing out how these portraits, too, are compounded of male wishes and fears more than of reality. For an example, the interested reader need only look at the journals of John Cheever, excerpted in *The New Yorker* in 1991. It is obvious that most of the portraits of the women he drew in his stories grew out of a very partial, needy, and narcissistic vision of his wife, Mary.

To ask "What is a true picture of a mother?" is to ask also "How do people come to know 'what is true'?" The answer narrative fiction poses to this basic human question is "point of view." As we look back over the literary history of our culture since *Don Quixote*, one thread is easy to discern, and that is the emergence into written literary voice of previously "voiceless" classes, nationalities, races, and affinity groups. It is not that these groups had not had a literature, which I define as a systematic way of looking at and analyzing the world through language, it is that the emergence of this "prepublished" literature into the sea of print can be dated. My favorite examples of this are the explosion of Russian literature at the beginning of the nineteenth century and the emergence of black American literature in the 1920s. Each of these changed the perception of "what is true" by giving eloquent voice to individual members of groups that had not been heard before, by bringing what had seemed alien into the realm of what the culture defined, through literary forms, as human. For the fact is that, through idiosyncratic voice and point of view, narrative literature highlights the experience of the individual, offers intimate contact with another experience, and circumvents the social differences that inspire hatred and alienation.

It means something, then, if mothers never speak in a literary voice, and if their sense of themselves as mothers and their view of those around them is not a commonplace of our written culture. It means, for one thing, that everyone in the culture is allowed, or even encouraged, to project all their conflicting fantasies, wishes, and fears onto the concept of motherhood, and onto their individual mothers and wives, which in turn creates of motherhood an ever-changing kaleidoscope of unrealistic and often conflicting aspirations and roles. Surely by now, for example, we are all familiar with the overlap in psychology's view of mothers between "coldness" and "overprotectiveness." There is, because these two categories overlap, no positive ground of "autonomy" and "loving-relatedness" that mothers can stand on. In the world of psychoanalysis, there is no space for mothers to have their own points of view about the demands their children make and whether these demands are realistic and able to be satisfied.

The failure of literature to include mothers also means that potential mothers, girls in adolescence who are often avid readers, have no variety in their models of mothering, and no model for articulating what it means to be a mother. Thus it is more likely that these girls will internalize those externally formulated projections of motherhood they find in their culture and discover, to their disappointment and frustration, that their "performance" as mothers is almost inevitably wanting. Such views are likely to be reinforced by the husband/father, who himself has no reality-based understanding of motherhood.

And the failure of literature to include mothers means that the delicate negotiation between responsibilities to self and to others, as represented by children and husband, but also by social networks of friends and co-workers, is never modeled for the culture at large. There are, certainly, many successful mothers who know themselves and their children, who understand the pleasures and the dangers of the world we live in, who make their way with courage and intelligence and good humor. Successful motherhood is a unique form of responsibility-taking, rooted in an understanding of competing demands, compromise, nurture, making the best of things, weighing often competing limitations, in order to arrive at a realistic mode of survival. A successful mother, we may imagine, is one who actually *looks at* her children and *sees* them, constantly weighing their potential against who they already seem to be, finding a balance that encourages them to live up to their best potential while not destroying them with impossible demands – while at the same time knowing the world they live in well enough to realistically judge how free they might be allowed to be without endangering themselves. Can a culture exist without such a strong model of responsible, realistic care?

Where were the mothers? Why *didn't* they speak up? Can mothers actually think and speak? If we look at Virginia Woolf and Vanessa Bell, it is the one who lived without sexual intimacy and without children who can't stop talking. Novels, essays, journals, letters – we are avid for everything she has to say. But the one who lived a passionate, sexual, child-bearing, and maternal life is, as far as the literary culture is concerned, dumb.

Others have written about the practical obstacles to mothers' writing – the pregnancies, the lack of day care, the myriad ways maternal responsibilities have fed into the already strong prohibitions against women writing. But I think there is something else. Perhaps one clue about maternal silence is in everyone's childhood memory of asking *Mom* who she loved best, asking her with anxiety and fear – she *might* say, or imply, she loved your brother best. You *might* detect in her tone evidence for your suspicion that such was the case. But there is also confidence, for this question is a ritual, and the ritual answers are "I love all of you the same," or "I love everybody as much as everybody else; I just love you in different ways." A reassuring answer. Surely, the child thinks, this can't be true. It isn't true of me. And yet *Mom* says over and over that it is true of her, so it must be true of her. Her love, unlike mine, is special, equal. It is *mother love*. The child is obscurely disappointed, too, because she senses that she hasn't gotten quite the truth. The effect, though, is that, as with anything simultaneously doubted and desired, mother love becomes something to be protected, never investigated, projected onto but never asked about or probed too deeply.

Where do mothers speak the truth? They speak it among themselves, over lunch or in groups. They laugh and confide, or cry and confide, that little Bobbie is driving them crazy, that Mary seems slower than the others, that (the greatest taboo) Angela isn't very pretty. They tell each other that Bob is too hard on the children and doesn't listen to them, and that it is clear that Bobbie's anger at this is approaching the breaking point. They ask each other what to do, and advise each other, on the understanding that judgment, in these conversations, is at least somewhat suspended in the common knowledge that everyone's kids give them trouble, and that if you judge me harshly now, I could return the favor in a year or two when your kid is arrested for drunk driving. Mothers, that is to say, *do* think, and they are very realistic and practical about mothering, but theirs is a literature, like the literature of Russia before the nineteenth century or of American blacks before the 1920s, that had not, when I became a mother, inserted itself very deeply into the print culture. To write about our own experience could lead us into, God forbid, analyzing our children and husbands, to belying the idea of maternal love that they depend upon. To write about the world could reveal in ourselves despair, alienation, fear, anomie that could communicate itself to our children and damage them.

Others have noticed the nonmaternal orientation of literary culture. In *Narrating Mothers: Theorizing Maternal Subjectivities,* editors Brenda Daly and Maureen Reddy note in their introduction the almost universal "daughter-centricity" of even feminist writing: "We most often hear daughters' voices in both literary and theoretical texts about mothers, mothering, and motherhood, even those written by feminists who are mothers . . . paying attention mostly to the effects of current conditions of mothering on children's progression into adulthood." Much of the reason for this, they suggest, is political: mothers are seen by many feminists as too implicated in the patriarchal power structure, or as too "limited" a group – to theorize about mothers is to exclude other women. Many feminist daughters define themselves in opposition to their own mothers, rejecting the compromises they have made and perhaps fearing, as well, the compromises they, the daughters, find themselves making. I submit another, in my view, more pertinent reason. Writing as a mother is simply too hard, even for mothers.

For the paradox of literary composition is that our work, even our most "realistic" work, is based on literary models. Life comes in as a corrective, but it is literature that tells us how to make literature. I experienced this very difficulty myself not too long ago. I had submitted to my publisher the rough drafts of my two novellas, *Ordinary Love* and *Good Will.* Each of these concerned a parent, a mother telling her story and a father telling his. And in each I wanted to use a form that would, I thought, be characteristically female or characteristically male. In fact, the male voice and his story – linear, suspenseful, full of cause and effect and action – came to me in one draft, and my editor demanded very few changes. *Ordinary Love* was much more difficult. The form I wanted to use was not linear. The most secret and dramatic section occurred halfway through, not at the normal time of climax. And the story was not complete, I thought, until the children's voices came back to the mother, until she had been forced to hear their responses to her assertions. And the fact is, it was not just that my editor was stubborn and, I thought, untrained to read this sort of text, it was that through many drafts I did not know what I was doing. I did not know how to make this unfolding form of secrets and surprises work. I was forced to write at the outer edges of my powers of *formal* invention, though I could actually hear my narrator's voice very clearly. The models for *Good Will* were all laid before me, as old and venerable as literature itself. The models for *Ordinary Love* were not even within me. I had to think them up as I went along. It was hard work.

But there is even more behind the "child-centricity" of literature than these points I have suggested. For the fact is that we approach literature, especially great literature, in the same way that children approach their parents. Everything about our education and our culture encourages us to do so. Shakespeare's phrases are embedded in the language, as if God-given. We identify certain names with greatness – Shakespeare, Milton, Melville, Austen – before we can make heads or tails of their writings. By the time we have begun to understand what they are saying, it has already taken on the color of universal truth, akin to phrases like "Round John Virgin" or "hollow be thy name" – it makes no sense but everybody honors it anyway. And western education is conducted very much on a religious model – we enter special places of learning, and listen to certified authorities interpreting the unchanging words of invisible and distant masters. We are told that while over in the scientific laboratories old findings and even theories are being superseded every day, here in the humanities buildings the truth doesn't change – the human spirit remains the same, a fascinating mix of good and evil and delineated, never again so profoundly, by those who have gone before. There are even those who maintain that the language has been, somehow, at least partially used up. Writers of the Renaissance, they say, had the benefit of a robust new language. The tired old language we have now will never express such passion again. This idea makes me think of families where Dad and all the kids are served, then Mom makes do with the heels of bread, the bones from the leg of lamb, and some deflowered stems of broccoli. There are even those who insist that authors do not exist. In this case, Mom belatedly answers her invitation, and discovers that the banquet is entirely over, the tables have been sent back to the caterers, and a vociferous number of the guests insists that no one even ate. Mom is obliged to take her hunger and go home.

Most writers who are not deconstructionists read the same way children do, receiving the truth from printed texts, allowing those truths to scour our souls and find them wanting, and the easiest thing in the world is then to *write* as children, following forms and rules that provide a well-marked path to greatness. Such a well-marked path we find, for example, in the disintegration and anomie of both modernism and postmodernism.

It is harder to write as an adult. However little we defer to our own parents or other authorities, it is still tempting to defer to the authorities of the literary world, and, if we teach, more than tempting to aggrandize ourselves by inculcating our students with belief in the greatness of the works we require them to read. But the trouble with greatness is that it seems to shade ineluctably into universality. When we assert that Shakespeare is the greatest writer of English, we can't seem to resist also asserting that his truths are the most universal. Another proposition that could be made, that his assertions are simply the most interesting and complex, doesn't satisfy our need to get next to the best, highest, and most important. Or, if we are of a different temperament, to deconstruct the best, highest, and most important.

What does this mean for mother/writers? To be an adult mother is, clearly, to have a vision that differs fundamentally in its experience and possibly in its expression from that of an adult father. We know this instinctively, and it doesn't matter if the cause of this difference is nature or nurture. It only matters that the difference exists. Additionally, an adult mother's vision offers a critique and a corrective on the vision of the father. Is there a family in the world where, when the kids complain about Dad, Mom does not offer some insight into his character, some perspective on his "universality"? Where she doesn't at least roll her eyes in quiet exasperation at certain absurd behaviors? Over a long marriage, Mom's vision offers a detached running commentary, equal in weight and significance to Dad's, whether that vision is expressed overtly or covertly. In fact, her very separateness from Dad asserts his particularity, his fallibility, the boundaries of his authority. To be an adult mother/writer would mean to challenge the universality of the themes present in "child-centric" and "father-centric" literatures, to challenge them perhaps without even knowing it, to challenge them as a natural result of one's carefully observed experience. Concomitantly, thinking about, questioning, discussing the experience of motherhood would develop this vision and its theory, as, over the last thousands of years, the patriarchal discourse has developed through the contributions of thousands of writers and critics.

What would such a vision contain? I give you the examples of Toni Morrison's *Beloved* and Sue Miller's *Family Pictures*. Two more different families than Sethe's family and the Eberharts would be hard to find, and yet the drama of each of these books revolves around the question of how to define mother love. In *Beloved,* Morrison makes a strong case for infanticide being the highest form of mother love in some circumstances. In *Family Pictures,* Miller gives the best answer I have ever heard to the "Who do you love best?" question. After Randall the autistic son dies, Lainey, the mother, and Nina, the sister closest in age to Randall, are talking. Lainey says, "Nina, no one gets love without some conditions. It's not in human nature to love that way, even your own children. You want certain things from them. You want certain things for them. I wish I could have loved you, all of you, that much. But's that's not in me. It's not in anyone." Nina says, "You loved Randall that way. Randall got that love." And Lainey says, "Oh, Nina, don't you think I wish I could have loved Randall with all those conditions? What a gift that would have been! It's the only kind I ever really wanted to feel. The other kind... who would want to feel it unless they had to?" Here is a vision of love to set beside all the myths of mother love – a love that is the particular expression of a particular personality and character, the idiosyncratic, real love of an imperfect self, not an impersonal, vapid ideal based on others' conflicting needs.

Surely another aspect of a mother's vision would be something that is another aspect of these novels: preoccupation with – insistence upon – survival, rather than the grand gesture of tragic death that ends so many masterpieces. There is, in western literature, what has to be interpreted as a refusal to go on, a willingness on the part of the larger heroes to vacate the mortal world through conflict, suicide, or a failure of the will to live. Need I add that there's always a mess to be cleaned up afterward that is not the concern of the dead tragic hero? A mother's vision would encompass survival, as it does in *Beloved* and *Family Pictures*, would encompass the cleaning up of messes.

But there is another question, as always: Can't we write about motherhood without having experienced it? The imagination, asserting its sole claim to power, cries "Yes!" but my experience, and the experience of other mother/writers – that what we have been feeling and doing as we have lived as mothers is *not* familiar, is in fact something that we had not been prepared for by our reading – contradicts the claim of the imagination. The paradox is that I have found it easier to write from the point of view of fathers than from the point view of mothers. I have, in fact, found it harder to sift through and understand my experience as a mother than to understand my husband's experience as a father because I have repeatedly felt the absence of a theory of motherhood formulated and thrashed out by other mothers, and the theories of motherhood formulated by psychology have simply felt wrong, and irrelevant, if not destructive.

Times have changed, and they have changed since I was first beginning to write not so long ago. Now the majority of women writers that I can think of have children, sometimes lots of children – not only Toni Morrison, Sue Miller, and Alice Walker, but also Louise Erdrich, Francine Prose, Sharon Olds, Maxine Hong Kingston, Maxine Kumin, Diane Johnson, Cynthia Ozick, Joy Williams, Meg and Hilma Wolitzer, Alice Munro, Alicia Ostriker, Grace Paley. And these writers often write about motherhood. It is no accident that this is a list of many who are generally acknowledged to be the most interesting writers of our time. Am I asking you to infer that a new literature, the literature of real, live motherhood, is inserting itself in our time, into the literary stream? You bet. Am I asking you to infer that it is as new and important in its way as any other new literature has been? You bet. For while the feminists are arguing whether motherhood is politically correct, and male novelists are worrying, as they have been at least all of my life, that the novel is dying, and the critics are asserting that the novel is deeply corrupt and the authors are dead, the mothers are busily, energetically, and prolifically exploring undiscovered territory within our own psyches, and therefore within the psyches of our readers, who are, as some of the letters I get attest, embarrassingly grateful. Have these mothers hammered out a consistent and self-conscious new vision yet? I don't know. I suspect it is too early to say. But they have revealed worlds that are new and old at the same time, worlds that we have never read about before but that we know are true.

And so I gave birth to my child, and Kafka hadn't affected her at all. I also, I found, gave birth to my subject, not the adventures of motherhood à la *Please Don't Eat the Daisies*, but the implications of daily power – the way in which one's sense of virtue, and desire to be good and innocent, conflicts with the daily exercise of power over the child. I never understood the interplay of love and power before I had children. I never knew what it felt like to have my actions magnified so enormously by the dependency of another. The intensity of my feelings, both positive and negative, was a certified surprise to me. In bad times, the strength I found to maintain some kind of stable routine, the faith I had in the simple value of survival, all of this came to me through my children. The shortest way of saying it is that motherhood is not a simple madonna picture, or a simple witch picture, but a hugely profound, complex, and, most importantly for a writer, *interesting* mix of evolving forces that challenge and change the self and the world. Imagining motherhood opens the door to imagining every power relationship, every profound connection. After my children were born, I felt, almost as a physical sensation, the nexus of their conflicting wishes, hopes, needs. Far from depriving me of thought, motherhood gave me new and startling things to think about and the motivation to do the hard work of thinking. For me, much of that thinking has been done through narrative fiction.

I have to admit that someone has suffered in the process, and it's been Kafka. While I am still deeply moved by much of his work, especially "The Metamorphosis," I now see it as fascinating but particular, *his* vision, not mine, many-layered and humanly recognizable, but masculine in some irreducible way, Shakespeare (should I whisper?), too. Even Dickens, my old favorite. Nor do I accept universality, and its partner simplicity, as a concept. Nor do I any longer wholly accept modernism. What I substitute is a picture of many women in a room, exchanging anecdotes of pregnancy and childbirth, all anecdotes simultaneously the same and different, the multifarious and the simple, the One and the many, existing together without cancelling each other out. To me that is the particular and complex vision of life that by and large is missing from our culture, whose absence has led us to invest our substance in religious fanaticism, crop monoculture, capitalistic gigantism, political and military conquest, aggrandizement of the self above everything and everyone else. It is a vision that, if we can insert it into the stream of literature, may help our culture to pause so we can save ourselves and the world that cradles us after all.

GARY SNYDER

Nature's Writing

[ART OF THE WILD CONFERENCE]

"Nature writing" has become a genre of increased literary interest recently. "Nature," has come to engage a number of artists and writers. This interest may be another function of postmodernism, since the modernist avant-garde was strikingly urban-centered. Many would-be nature writers approach this territory in a mode of curiosity, respect, and concern, without necessarily seeking literary reputation. They are doing it for love and the eco-warrior's passion, not for money. (There is still a wide range of views and notions about what nature writing ought to be. The older sort of nature writing was largely from a human perspective; and much of it middle-class, middlebrow Euro-American at that. It has a rhetoric of beauty, harmony, and sublimity. What makes us uncomfortable sometimes with John Muir's writing is an excess of these sentiments. He had contemporaries now forgotten who were far worse.)

Natural history writing is another branch: semiscientific, objective, in the descriptive mode. Both the above sorts of writing are "naïvely realistic" in that they unquestioningly accept the front-mounted bifocal human eye, the poor human sense of smell, and other characteristics of our species – and the idea that the mind can, without much self-examination, directly and objectively "know" whatever it looks at. There has also always been a certain amount of heroic journal and narrative literature of exploration and exploitation, and more recently the writings of wilderness recreation and adventure. And there is an old mix of science, nature appreciation, and conservation politics that has been a potent part of the evolution of the conservation movement in the United States. The best of this can be seen in the work of Rachel Carson and Aldo Leopold. All the above might be seen by some as mildly anthropocentric, but all of it is worthy and goodhearted. We are in its debt.

Nature writing has been held in less than full esteem by the literary establishment. I think this is because it was focused on something other than the subject matter of mainstream occidental writing, namely the moral quandaries, competitions, affairs of the heart, and soul-searchings of highly gifted and often powerful people, usually male. Tales of the elites. In fact, up until a decade ago most nature writing was relegated to a status not unlike that of women's writings: it was seen as a writing of sensibility and empathy and observation, but off to the side, not really serious, not important.

If we look at the longer time-frame of occidental culture, even with its educated elites, and literary culture, it can be seen that the natural world is profoundly present in many of the great works of art. The human experience has been played out in intimate relationship to the natural world. This is even too obvious to say, yet it is often oddly forgotten. History, philosophy, and literature naturally foreground human affairs, social dynamics, questions, intellectual constructs. A critical subtheme that runs through it all has to do with defining the human relation to the rest of nature. In our earlier literature nature provides not only the background and the scene, but also many of the characters. The "classical" world of myth is a world in which animal beings, supernatural figures, and humans are actors and interacters. Bears, bulls, and swans were not abstractions to the people of earlier times, but real creatures in very real landscapes. The auroch – the giant wild cow, *Bos,* who became Zeus to "Europa" – survived in pockets in the European forests until medieval times.

As I have said elsewhere, we have been living on a planet on which human populations were relatively small, and on which human travel took place on foot, by horse, or by sail. Whether in Greece, Germania, or Han China, there were always nearby areas of forest, wild animals, migratory waterfowl, seas full of fish and whales, in the experience of every aware person. Animals as characters in literature and archetypes in religion are there for the very concrete reason of their nearby existence and powerful presence in the human imagination. Ideas and feelings about wastelands, wildernesses, and mountains are not born of abstraction, but of real places that must be traversed while traveling cisalpine, hyperboreal, beyond the pale, or whatever. This is the world people lived in up until the late nineteenth century: plentiful wildlife, open space, small human population, trails instead of roads – and human lives of individual responsibility and existential intensity. This is not "frontier" that we're considering, but the normal daily life of our ancestors. It is also the Holocene era, our *present* era, in all its glory of salmon, bear, elk, deer, and moose. Where do the sacred salmon of the Celts, the Bjorns and Brauns and Brun-(hilde) [*bher*–bear]s of northern European literature, the dolphins of the Mediterranean, the bear-dances of Artemis, the lion-skin of Herakles, come from but the wild systems the humans lived near? –

> those images that yet
> fresh images beget
> that dolphin torn, that
> gong-tormented sea.
>
> –William Butler Yeats

Nonetheless many notables in the literary establishment are not enthralled with the natural world, and indeed some still resent or fear it. Take this quote from Howard Nemerov, a good poet and a decent man: "Civilization, mirrored in language, is the garden where relations grow; outside the garden is the wild abyss."

The unexamined assumptions here are fascinating. They are – at worst – crystallizations of the erroneous views that enable the developed world to displace third- and fourth-world peoples and overexploit nature globally. The point is here proposed that language is somehow implicitly civilized or civilizing, that civilization is orderly, that intrahuman relations are the pinnacle of experience (as though all of us, and all life on the planet, were not interrelated), and that "wild" means "abyssal," disorderly, and chaotic.

First, take language. Some theorists have latched on to "language" as that which somehow makes us different. They have the same enthusiasm for the "Logos" as the old Summer Institute of Linguistics for bible translation into unwritten languages. Any current writer who doesn't know what else to say about her work – when asked to give a sound bite –

has declared, "Well, I'm just fascinated with language." The truth is language is part and parcel of consciousness, and we know virtually nothing about either one. Our study and respect should extend to them both.

On another tack, the European deconstructionists assume, because of their monotheistic background, that the Logos died along with God. Those who wish to de-center occidental metaphysics have begun to try to devalue both language and nature, and declare them both to be further inventions of ruling-class mythology. In the past, the idea that the external world was our own invention came out of some variety of idealist thought. But *this* version leads to a totally weird philosophical position that (since the proponents are at least in part intellectual Marxists) might be called "materialistic solipsism." But this is all talk.

There is a truly dangerous oxymoron heard in some fashionable but cynical business and government circles called "Sustainable Development." Development is not going to be easily compatible with biodiversity. We must drop talking about development, and concentrate on how to achieve a steady-state condition of real sustainability. Much economic development is simply the further extension of the destabilizing, entropic, and disorderly functions of industrial civilization.

So I am arguing, and have developed my argument elsewhere, that consciousness, mind, imagination, *and* language are fundamentally wild. "Wild" as in wild ecosystems – richly interconnected, interdependent, and incredibly complex. Diverse, ancient, and full of information. At root it is a question of how we understand the concepts of order, freedom, and chaos. Is art an imposition of order on chaotic nature, or is art (also read "language") a matter of discovering the grain, a matter of uncovering the intricate and nonsymmetrical order, of the processes that bring about the natural world? Observation, reflection, and practice show artistic processes to be the latter.

Our school in the mountains here at Squaw Valley is called "The Art of the Wild." (Incidentally, I was wondering just what edible root might have been growing so profusely in the wet bottoms of this valley, originally, to have caused it to be called "Squaw Valley." Any place named "squaw" is usually so named following on some white guys seeing numerous Native American women at work gathering wild food. Up here it might have been Brodeia bulbs. As though some native women coming on a Euro-American farming community had called it White Boy Flats.)

The "Art of the Wild" is to see art in the light of the process of nature –
nature *as* process rather than as product or commodity – because "wild" is
a name for the way that phenomena continually actualize themselves.
Seeing this also serves to acknowledge the autonomy and integrity of the
nonhuman part of the world, an "Other" that we are barely beginning to
be able to know. In disclosing, discovering, the wild world with our kind
of writing we may find ourselves breaking into unfamiliar territories that
do not reflect anything known as "nature writing" from the past. The
work of the art of the wild can well be irreverent, ugly, frazzled, unpredictable, simple and clear – or virtually inaccessible. Who will write of the
odd barbed, hooked, bent, splayed, and crooked penises of nonhuman
male creatures? Of sexism among spiders? Someone will yet come to
write with the eye of an insect, write from the undersea world, or find
other ways of writing that step outside the human.

As I have written in *The Practice of the Wild*,

Life in the wild is not just eating berries in the sunlight. I like to imagine a "depth
ecology" that would go to the dark side of nature – the ball of crunched bones in a
scat, the feathers in the snow, the tales of insatiable appetite. Wild systems are in
one elevated sense above criticism, but they can also been seen as irrational,
mouldy, cruel, parasitic. Jim Dodge told me how he had watched – with fascinated
horror – Orcas methodically batter a Gray whale to death in the Chukchee sea.
Life is not just diurnal and a property of large interesting vertebrates, it is also noc-
turnal, anaerobic, cannibalistic, microscopic, digestive, fermentative: cooking
away in the warm dark. Life is well maintained at a four-mile ocean depth, is waiting and sustained on a frozen rock wall, and clinging and nourished in hundred-
degree desert temperatures. And there is a world of nature on the decay side, a
world of beings who do rot and decay in the shade. Human beings have made
much of purity, and are repelled by blood, pollution, putrefaction. The other side
of the "sacred" is the sight of your beloved in the underworld, dripping with mag-
gots. Coyote, Orpheus, and Izanagi cannot help but look, and they lose her.
Shame, grief, embarrassment, and fear are the anaerobic fuels of the dark imagination. The less familiar energies of the wild world, and their analogs in the imagination, have given us ecologies of the imagination. . . .

Narratives are one sort of trace that we leave in the world. All our literatures are
leavings, of the same order as the myths of wilderness peoples who leave behind
only stories and a few stone tools. Other orders of beings have their own literatures. Narrative in the deer world is a track of scents that is passed on from deer to

deer, with an art of interpretation which is instinctive. A literature of blood-stains, a bit of piss, a whiff of estrus, a hit of rut, a scrape on a sapling, and long gone. And there might be a "narrative theory" among these other beings – they might ruminate on "intersexuality" or "decomposition criticism."

I propose this to turn us loose to think about "wild writing" without preconception or inhibition, but at the same time with craft. The craft could be seen as the swoop of a hawk, the intricate galleries of burrowing and tunneling done by western pine bark beetles, the lurking-at-the-bottom of a big old trout, the kamikaze sting of a yellowjacket, the insouciant waddle of a porcupine, the constant steadiness of a flow of water over a boulder, the chatter of a squirrel, the crazy calls of screech owls in the night. Images of our art. Nature's writing has the potential of becoming the most radical, fluid, transgressive, pansexual, subductive, and morally vital kind of writing on the scene. In becoming so it may help halt one of the most terrible things of our time – the destruction of species and their habitats, the elimination of some living beings forever.

Finally: let us not get drawn too far into dichotomous views and arguments about civilization versus nature, the domesticated versus the wild, the garden versus the wild abyss. Creativity itself is wildness, and wildness is freedom, and freedom is the ability to live in the real physical daily world at each moment, totally and completely.

CHRISTOPHER MERRILL

Regained Detachment: On Thomas Mann, Gabriel García Márquez, and the New World Order

[YALE ENVIRONMENTAL WRITING CONFERENCE]

My idea of Venice, it is true, was conditioned by repeated readings of Thomas Mann's *Death in Venice*. His short novel was my literary bible when I started writing, a book I studied for its technical merits as well as for its aesthetic truth, a cautionary tale whose stern admonishments about the dangers of fame and single-mindedness I heed to this day. Gustav von Aschenbach's dissolution amidst "the feasts of the sun," the city's languorous ways, the determination with which the Venetians – and the famous writer – ignore or cover up the spread of typhus, the unspoken threat of world war articulating itself in the distance: these were the individual notes of a chord that never ceased to thrill me.

"Solitude," Mann writes, "gives birth to the original in us, to beauty unfamiliar and perilous – to poetry. But also, it gives birth to the opposite: to the perverse, the illicit, the absurd." Certainly as a young writer I understood some of the hazards associated with solitude, which I both yearned for and feared. And Venice represented that two-edged sword I had honed in my twenties. Thus when I had the chance to visit that city I felt as if, on at least one level, I was making a pilgrimage to the birthplace of my own literary sensibility.

Writers can justify anything in the name of their art – a central point in Mann's work – and I am no exception. Explaining away my two-day excursion to Venice was simple: after an arduous month on the trail of a new book about the Balkans, I told myself I needed a break. I had interviewed scores of writers, artists, political figures, and the like in Slovenia; hiked across two mountain ranges; and collected so many impressions that I had more than one hundred pages of notes and a thick callus on the index finger of my writing hand. How does raw experience translate into story? Perhaps I would discover something about that mysterious process if I left my notebooks in Ljubljana and traveled to the spiritual home of numbers of Slovenes. Venice, after all, bears the same relationship to the northernmost republic of what was once Yugoslavia that a novel's scenes and descriptions do to its plot: the pilings on which the city is slowly sinking into the sea come from trees cut down in the Kaarst region of Slovenia. Nina Zagoricnik, the radio journalist who was to drive me to Venice, had said that "Slovenia is possible only as long as one thinks constantly of Italy." Now I might find out why.

Joseph Brodsky calls Venice "a work of art, the greatest masterpiece our species has produced." No doubt I needed to be reminded of the rich sources of invention and imagination man occasionally taps. For the last month I had confronted again and again fresh evidence of our ability to commit unspeakable horrors. A three-day hike through the Pohorje Mountains in northeastern Slovenia had become as much an exercise in historical memory as a trek through an indescribably beautiful and varied landscape. Here, among thick forests and an alpine bogland, tidy farms and cascading waterfalls, chapels and hunters' stands, were shrines commemorating the partisans who in World War II had fought off the Nazis. Near the end of our journey, after my companion and I had shouted with joy at the orderly splendor of a high mountain meadow that men with scythes and sickles had cut by hand, we came to a lodge filled with refugees from Bosnia, victims of the Serbian "ethnic cleansing" campaign; the converted military barracks in the valley were full.

Slovenia had emerged intact from its ten-day war with Serbia. Yet there were signs everywhere of Yugoslavia's continuing troubles – 100,000 refugees scattered around the newly independent nation, families of Gypsies on street corners in Ljubljana, news of more atrocities in Bosnia. One night I wandered, in shock and horror, through an exhibition of photographs Jana Schneider had taken in Sarajevo. She was an American photojournalist who had nearly lost her life in a bombing three months earlier; her lover, also a photographer, had not been so fortunate. The Serbs firing on Sarajevo, it was widely believed, were targeting journalists to scare them away. Their tactics had not worked with Schneider, who was working to bring the war in Bosnia to the world's attention – despite having twenty-two holes and forty pieces of shrapnel in her body. She could barely walk, and still she had produced a show whose images I would not forget – buildings reduced to rubble, overturned cars, bodies stretched out on sidewalks, a cat in its death throes. In Sarajevo, I learned that night, there are SNIPER WARNING signs on the streets; every adult bears bruises from diving to the ground to avoid being shot.

Nor were the wounds limited to the physical. Only the day before I was to leave for Venice I interviewed Harris Burina, Sarajevo's leading actor, who was then waiting for a visa to Paris. He was a man without a country: having acted for the previous year with a troupe in Belgrade, he was persona non grata in his home town, and because he was a Muslim from Bosnia, the Serbs too were aiming for him. Before leaving for Slovenia, Burina had been reduced to waiting tables in a pizzeria. The diners kept looking for cameras; this had to be a movie set, and their favorite actor was shooting a new film. Burina had told this story with relish, then his expression changed. "All I have left," he said sadly, "is my wife and my memories." Judging from the harshness with which he addressed his wife whenever she interrupted him – they had drunk seven bottles of wine after lunch the day before, and now they were suffering from terrible hangovers – I could believe that soon he might have only memories.

Now I was on my way to a city awash in memory. At the border we were stopped and searched three different times; two days earlier an Italian relief plane had been shot down over Sarajevo, and the *carabinieri* were taking extra precautions to stop the smuggling of Bosnians into their country. Slovenia, my friends had said, was being turned into a *cordon sanitaire;* no Western European country wanted more refugees. At last we came to Venice, boarded what Nina called a *fairy tale*, and headed up the Grand Canal and across the water to the Lido, the site of the film festival she would report on for Radio Slovenia. I took a room in the Hotel Hungaria, which despite its outward appearance of gentility and the high prices of its rooms was little more than a fleabag, and arranged to meet

Nina in the morning, when she would interview Gabriel García Márquez, a distinguished guest of the festival.

I looked forward to that interview. At sunset I strolled down the beach past teenagers playing soccer, families packing up their belongings, a long line of cabanas, a couple making love in the sand, old men fishing from the stone jetty leading out to the lighthouse. The war in Bosnia? A world away from here. I thought of questions I might ask the Colombian novelist, who was one of my literary heroes: how, for example, does one juggle the imperatives of fiction-writing with a career as a journalist, especially within our so-called new world order? Ryszard Kapuscinski recently said that "it is very difficult to write now, because the end of our century is marked by a tremendous acceleration of the historical process. Literature hates this." He went on to remark that

> The writer needs a certain quietness and evenness of perspective, a space of time for reflection. There is no distance now. There are some changes that we can watch on the television, but there are certain very profound, important transformations which we do not have the opportunity to see. Fiction writers avoid this by writing about marriage, love, things like that; they will not touch the volcano the world has become.
>
> If you try to touch it, to describe it, you find that it requires a new imagination. The problem is not so much with the writing itself as with the creative imagination. The acceleration of history proves that we have a very limited imaginary capacity. We never dreamed that the world would become such a rich and various place.

I wondered how García Márquez might respond to Kapuscinski's line of reasoning—an attitude echoed in my interviews with any number of Slovene writers. "We need a new language," I kept hearing in Ljubljana, "with which to address the way the world is changing." If any novelist might parse that knowledge, I told myself as I walked back into town, it was the author of *One Hundred Years of Solitude*. I remembered that his American editor had spent his honeymoon at my house in Santa Fe, and I had heard enough stories about him to imagine that in certain ways I almost knew him. How many writers had he inspired to use all available resources—imaginative, linguistic, and political—to further the cause of freedom! Nina particularly wanted him to offer words of hope for her countrymen, who were staring, as I so often heard, "into the abyss of Bosnia."

I ate dinner at an outdoor café, where over a bottle of the local white wine I reread *Death in Venice*. Perhaps because I had spent the last month among writers convinced that the west's failure to intervene on behalf of the Bosnians amounted to a kind of appeasement not witnessed on the Continent since the 1930s, I was more than ordinarily struck by Mann's description of Aschenbach's central work, *The Abject:*

> With rage the author here rejects the rejected, casts out the outcast – and the measure of his fury is the measure of his condemnation of all moral shilly-shallying. Explicitly he renounces sympathy with the abyss, explicitly he renounces the flabby humanitarianism of the phrase: *"Tout comprendre c'est tout pardonner."* What was here unfolding, or rather was already in full bloom, was the "miracle of regained detachment," which a little later became the theme of one of the author's dialogues, dwelt upon not without a certain oracular emphasis. Strange sequence of thought! Was it perhaps an intellectual consequence of this rebirth, this new austerity, that from now on his style showed an almost exaggerated sense of beauty, a lofty purity, symmetry, and simplicity, which gave his productions a stamp of the classic, of conscious and deliberate mastery? And yet: this moral fibre, surviving the hampering and disintegrating effect of knowledge, does it not result in its turn in a dangerous simplification, in a tendency to equate the world and the human soul, and thus to strengthen the hold of the evil, the forbidden, and the ethically impossible?

I was a little drunk, yet I was convinced that the biggest threat in our new world order was "dangerous simplification." Politicians, I well knew, were not the only specialists in reducing complicated situations and ideas to slogans and sound bites. I slept fitfully that night.

In the morning we drove to the Hotel Excelsior to pick up García Márquez. Nina parked in a no-parking zone, and while she went into the lobby to call him, I stayed in the car to keep it from being towed away. Minutes later I was shaking hands with the Nobel laureate, a handsome man in a bold blue shirt and a white sport jacket. In the *Paris Review* interview Nina had used to prepare for her own interview, he had been likened to "a good middleweight fighter – broad-chested, but perhaps a bit thin in the legs." Ten years later, the description still held, and I was too dazzled to say anything more than my name by way of introduction. He smiled, and soon we were driving to the Hôtel des Bains, where Aschenbach had stayed in Mann's novel and where García Márquez was to take part in a large panel discussion connected with the festival.

"Nous parlons en Français," Nina said as we drove by the sea, *"parce que c'est la langue nous pouvons parler ensemble."*

"Biens," I said, nodding, then listened to her ask him several questions, which he answered pleasantly until she turned around and asked me, in English, if I knew the French word for the pine trees lining both sides of the road. "I can't remember," I said with a shrug. Nina went on with her questioning, but now García Márquez refused to answer her. He was clearly upset. He did not say another word. And when we came to the hotel, he got out of the car, slammed the door shut, and marched off in silence. Nina looked at me, puzzled, then chased after him. He turned to her, she would tell me once we were inside the lobby, and said, "I hate Americans. No interview." Then he walked away.

Inside the hotel ballroom, an elaborate room featuring a pair of chandeliers, ornately carved wooden pillars, and thick red curtains hanging from the balcony, were more than six hundred journalists waiting for the panel to begin. Cameramen filmed the crowd, reporters adjusted their headphones to hear the translators, and security officers with cellular phones scanned the list of speakers. "They all have beautiful women," Nina said of the men approaching the tables arranged behind the lectern, studying themselves in the mirrors embedded in the pillars surrounding the room. García Márquez, Wim Wenders, Peter Handke, Costa-Gavras, Dennis Hopper, Sean Penn – these were just some of the more than fifty luminaries invited to address the burning issue of the day. I pushed my ugly encounter with the Nobel laureate out of my mind and leaned forward to hear what his colleagues had to say.

I assumed that the subject of the panel would be the siege of Sarajevo and the failure of the west to stop the slaughter of innocents. We were too close to the fighting to avoid discussing it, and here were some of the most famous *engagé* artists of our time gathering to speak out. It was García Márquez, after all, who had said in his *Paris Review* interview that "the only advantage of fame is that I have been able to give it a political use." Surely this panel, which would include Italian president Paolo Portoghesi, France's flamboyant minister of culture Jack Lang, and Lina

Wertmuller, would not shirk its moral responsibilities.

I was, of course, wrong. One speaker after another rose to his or her feet to condemn America for its failure to honor an artist's "moral rights." It seemed that the U.S. government had not complied with the "moral rights" provisions of the Bern Treaty, the world's copyright standard; filmmakers in our country had no protection against studios tampering with their work. George Lucas, according to *Variety*, had painted an "Orwellian future" for his industry. "Releasing entities," he had asserted six months earlier, "have gained experience through the video market and colorization, and it's not going to be too long in the future before an actor, who has become unacceptable for whatever reason of politics or marketability, might be in the future electronically replaced by another actor." And the speakers in the ballroom of the Hôtel des Bains repeated his warning that soon "the theme of a motion picture might be altered to achieve whatever politically correct or economically driven objective its owners wish to impose."

Who could argue with that? Nevertheless, after two hours of listening to the artists' harangue, I grew more and more impatient. This was overkill. I could not help thinking that this panel had, like the European Community and the Bush Administration, missed a chance to deal with the most pressing issue of the post–Cold War world. I tried to imagine what it had cost the organizers of the film festival to bring together these speakers: hundreds of thousands of dollars. I listened to the passion with which each artist spoke, and I found myself becoming angrier by the minute. Aschenbach had lost his bearings in Mann's fictionalized version of this setting, inflamed with his desire for the forbidden – a Polish boy who would not "likely live to grow old." I remembered a sentence I had underlined the night before in my copy of *Death in Venice:* "For in almost every artist nature is inborn a wanton and treacherous proneness to side with the beauty that breaks hearts, to single out aristocratic pretensions and pay them homage." How many films, tawdry and serious, had broken my heart. How often had I paid homage to aristocratic pretensions and thus lost sight of the truth of my experiences in the world. I had had enough of the Venice Film Festival. I walked out into the sunshine and down the beach until I came to a deserted stretch of sand, where I stripped off my clothes and dove into the sea.

Nina, as it turned out, eventually convinced García Márquez to do a brief interview – on condition that he not be asked any questions about Yugoslavia, a situation he did not understand. Ten years earlier, on the eve of winning the Nobel Prize, he had concluded his *Paris Review* interview with an optimistic prediction about his future work: "I'm absolutely convinced that I'm going to write the greatest book of my life, but I don't know which one it will be or when. When I feel something like this – which I have been feeling now for awhile – I stay very quiet so that if it passes by I can capture it." Nina rounded off her interview with him by asking if he still felt that way. "No," he said sadly.

JULIAN GLOAG

Talking to the Horse

[PARIS WRITERS' WORKSHOP]

There is a short story by Chekhov, written I suppose in the eighties or nineties of the last century, about an old cab driver in Moscow one night in the depths of winter. While he waits patiently for fares, he sits, hunched up against the extreme cold, and ruminates about his son, also a cab driver, who died the day before. It is a long wait, but at last he gets a fare, who wants to be taken to the opera house. When they have gone a little way on the packed snow – the cab is a sledge – the old man turns to his fare and says, "My son died yesterday..."

"No doubt he did," says the fare, "and I'm sorry for it, but if you don't get a move on, the curtain will have gone up."

The next fare, after another long wait, is going to a large hotel, and to him too the driver says, "You know, my son died yesterday."

"Well, well," is the reply, "we all have to die sometime. Now whip up that wretched horse of yours, I'm already late."

The driver drops him at the hotel and stays there, hoping for another fare. After a minute or two, the hotel doorman comes across to him. "My son died yesterday," says the old man.

"I daresay he did," says the doorman, "too bad, but you can't wait here, you know – so be off with you!"

Finally, late, when there are no more fares to be had, the old man returns to the dormitory where the cab drivers sleep. He stables his horse and goes into the dormitory and sits down by the stove. One of the sleeping drivers wakes up and comes to get a glass of water. The old man says, "Yesterday my son died..."

"Oh yes?" says the other driver with a yawn. "If you're asking me, he's well out of it." And he totters back to bed.

The old man would like to speak about it all – how his son fell ill and sickened and was taken to the hospital, and what the doctor said and what his son said at the end and how he died. But there is no one willing to listen. So in the end he gets up and goes into the stable and tells the whole story to his little horse.

Well, here we are, a whole collection of storytellers, anxious and eager to tell our stories – but who's listening? We used to be able to be confident – certainly when I started writing novels thirty-some years ago – that a good, decently written book (of *whatever* kind) had a very fair chance of being published, reviewed, and read by some sort of public on its merits as a piece of writing, as a story. It may still happen – with luck. But all too often the luck depends on a turn of fashion, a gimmick, a trick, a hype-able personality, and has not much to do with the actual quality of the work.

For instance, if I were to shoot my publisher in some nice public place with plenty of blood, I guarantee all my novels would be back in print in plenty of time for the trial – irresistible publicity (and free!). And who knows, it might start a trend, and the world would be a lot better off. Let's start with Rupert Murdoch.

Actually, my (English) publisher is a very nice man indeed and I wouldn't dream of killing him. He said to me once that there are three types of publisher: one who likes books but not authors, one who likes authors but not books, and one who likes both books and authors. Christopher is of the third type. Three years ago, he founded his own independent publishing house in order to publish the books *he* liked. Three months ago, he sold out to a conglomerate in order to avoid bankruptcy. He was almost certainly the last of the gentleman publishers in London – a breed that has long died out in New York. For, of course, there is a fourth breed of publisher: the publisher who likes neither books nor authors, doesn't read the one and seldom meets the other unless it happens to be an ex-president or a movie star. And this is the predominant type of publisher today.

Why? Erica Jong, now president of the Authors Guild, put it like this in a recent speech: "What has happened to publishing in the last twenty years? Giant conglomerates (for whom authors are merely software) have been buying up publishing houses since the 1960s. As a result, belles lettres, history, poetry, and risky new books by risky new authors have become an endangered species. The scene has gotten grimmer and grimmer."

There is a rather grim story about Bennett Cerf, who was one of the very first to sell out to a conglomerate. When he sold Random House to RCA, he was assured there would be no policy changes and he was allowed to stay on as president. After a couple of years in which he saw many of his old authors turned away, contracts arbitrarily canceled, two thirds of the backlist of the Modern Library swept away – he resigned. Not long after, he went to stay with some friends in the country; one morning, his host, who was an early riser, went to take a dip and heard, coming from the small copse that screened the pool from the house, a curious noise. It was Bennett Cerf, sitting on a garden bench, sobbing. "Why, Bennett, what in the world's the matter?"

"Oh, why did I do it?" said the weeping Cerf. "Why on earth did I do it?"

But weep not for Bennett Cerf. He *did* it. They all did it – Dutton, Simon & Schuster, Secker and Warburg, Heinemann, Hamish Hamilton, Sinclair-Stevenson, just to name those of my own taken-over publishers from whom I have received elaborate letters promising that nothing would change. But of course it did change, has changed. Now most sizable firms are controlled by corporate accountants for whom books are merely merchandise, whose only reading matter is the profit and loss sheet, and whose eyes are firmly fixed on the bottom line, which does not read "And they all lived happily ever after" but is printed in little black figures. And the problem is that those figures have to be very black. In other words, every book is measured as a potential best-seller. And one best-seller is more profitable than a dozen books that sell three or four thousand copies and don't get into mass-market paperback, though they may break even or perhaps make a small profit. So to the mind of the accountant there is simply no point in publishing those twelve books (he is, of course, even on his own terms, absurdly shortsighted, because one of them might turn out to be a winner).

Obviously there still are individual editors, quite a lot of them, even in the conglomerate publishing houses, who are still in the business for love. But gone are the days when they could simply walk into the editorial conference and say, "I love this book and I want to publish it." Editors used to have to balance in their minds three things: the quality of the work, its commercial prospects, and their faith in the author. Faith in – or loyalty to – the author is a laughable concept today. And when the quality of the work is a minor consideration (over against its supposed commercial prospects in reaching a publishing decision), what happens is a subtle corruption of even the best of editorial minds. Even intelligent and sensitive editors (and agents, it must be said), forced to think in solely commercial terms, have their taste degraded and their judgment impaired. And I am by no means talking only about "literary" works.

Why, for instance, is it so almighty difficult to find a good thriller these days? Where are the Chester Himeses and Robert Gullicks of yesteryear? Why are we forced back to reread Raymond Chandler and Georges Simenon and Amanda Cross? Look around and you will find, not that every cloud is silver-lined, but that all paperbacks are stamped with silver – and lustrous, bloody red and gold. Fools' gold. Not so long ago I was standing next to a couple of businessmen at the bookstall in Heathrow Airport who were looking sadly at the paperback display. One said, "I've read the lot." The other said, with a sigh, "Well, if you've read one, you've read them all." He might better have said, "If you've read them all, you've read one." Because, in effect, they are all the same book: pseudo-Forsyth, pseudo-Francis, pseudo-Forester, even, Lord save us, pseudo-Ken Follet (known to the trade, owing to his overmastering predilection for money, as Ken Wallet). This is not the authors' fault – the accountant/controller, elated with one success, believes in formula repetition. And in a commercial sense, maybe he's not wrong. That's the appalling thing. In my brief career as an encyclopedia salesman, I learned that the best sales prospect was someone who had already bought the encyclopedia – "Ah, well, of course, Mrs. Robinson, then you know its value . . . " Once, alas, a sucker, always a sucker.

"Drive on, drive on!" says the publisher. "Write on, write on. Flog the old horse – speed it up or we'll miss the market!"

Publishers are not interested in the telling of your grief, in the story of your heart, in matters of life and death. They are like the deaf adder that stoppeth her ear, which will not hearken to the voice of charmers, charming never so wisely. They want you to repeat the same thing, over and over again (although, curiously enough, when I actually wrote a novel called *The Same Thing,* they were horrified and insisted I change the title).

Well, the publishers are not listening – because they are not reading, or have forgotten how to read, and if they do publish your book and your book is at all complicated, as likely as not they haven't the faintest idea of what they've got. In this respect, publishing has become more and more like Hollywood. (I remember when James B. Harris bought the movie rights to my second novel, he called me up. "Julie, baby," he said, "I love it! Tell me – what's it about?")

Well, so, who else? The academics – are they listening?

In an essay on George Orwell, written in 1951, Lionel Trilling recalled how, at the moment he had decided to write the piece, one of his graduate students came in to announce that he, too, had decided to write an essay on Orwell. Amused and pleased by the coincidence, they began to chat about their common subject:

> But I asked him not to talk about Orwell. I didn't want to dissipate in talk what ideas I had, and also I didn't want my ideas crossed with his, which were sure to be very good. So for a while we merely exchanged bibliographical information, asking each other which of Orwell's books we'd read and which we owned. But then, as if he could not resist making at least one remark about Orwell himself, he said suddenly in a very simple and matter-of-fact way, "he was a virtuous man." And we sat there, agreeing at length about this statement, finding pleasure in talking about it.
>
> It was an odd statement for a man to make nowadays, and I suppose that what we found so interesting about it was just this oddity – its point was in its being an old-fashioned thing to say.

If it was an odd and old-fashioned statement to make even then, forty years ago, today it would be inconceivable. I doubt whether George Orwell is much read in universities these days. The present president of the Modern Language Association, which has close to thirty thousand members – thirty thousand professors of literature! – is a scholar who has campaigned for the replacement of the present literary "canon" with a canon consisting wholly of black women writers. Wonderful for black women writers, but not so hot for the rest of us.

Of course the argument isn't that these writers are more valuable than other writers – value is irrelevant; what is truly relevant is power. Just as political correctness dismisses "value" or "quality," so the deconstructionists have replaced "works" with "texts." A text is a corpse you dissect; a work is a live thing to laugh or cry at. And as the work disappears, so does the author, he is a total irrelevance (and is taken to know nothing about his own work – incidentally, an attitude shared by quite a few editors).

Frank Kermode, who is firmly of the old humanist guard, has written that:

> The entire operation of high-powered literary criticism ultimately depends on the preservation of the reading public without which literature cannot exist. University teachers of literature can read what they like, and deconstruct and neo-historicize what they like, but in the classroom they should be on their honour to make people know books well enough to understand what it is to love them. If they fail in that, either because they despise the humbleness of the task or because they don't themselves love literature, they are failures and frauds.

This is strong stuff. Normally, I don't think writers should pay the slightest attention to what academics say or think – listening to them can make you feel small and confused or self-important and grand, either of which gets between you and your work, if you let it. Nevertheless, at the very back of our minds is perhaps the feeling that academics are useful, that one day, when we are long dead and gone, it is they who will carry us down to posterity. This no longer seems even a remote possibility. The academics are working hard to deprive us not only of present readership, but also of readers to come. It's not just that they don't like books and don't like authors, that, like the hotel doorman, they are saying to us, "You can't wait here – be off with you," because there are big things going on inside the hotel (maybe the annual MLA conference) and the last person they want in there is a writer. They also are contemptuous of the past and, surely most devastating of all, they don't love the truth. This really hits where it hurts – especially if you agree with Chekhov that, fundamentally, the only reason for writing is to tell the truth.

To teach that truth doesn't matter or that there is no truth or that all truths are equal (though some are more equal than others – i.e., "mine for the moment") has a shattering effect on the confidence of those being taught. You can see this, I think, in the way that students – and not just students – are tentative about everything they say. They make even the simplest of statements sound like a question: "I went to the movies last night? I saw this film? The one about these two women? In the car?" And if they are saying something that begins to sound too downright or if they are challenged in any way, they tend to say "it really doesn't matter. . . . " Intellectual appreciation is expressed by "Well, yeah, I'm comfortable with that." My mother used to get particularly exasperated at the table by people who, when asked whether they wanted a second helping, would reply "I'm happy, thanks." She would say snappishly, "I didn't ask you how you were, I asked you whether you wanted any more to *eat!*" Just so, one wants to say, "I don't care about your comfort – I'm asking you what you *think!*"

The point is of course that they don't *know* what they think: they haven't been trained to think. And they hardly know what they feel, because they haven't been allowed to react naturally. And even when, despite this, they *do* have a strong reaction, they don't know or are not sure or are afraid to express an opinion. They have lost the ability to take simple pleasure in a story. They have to be reassured that it's okay to like something. I recently received a letter from a reader in California – actually three letters because he sent it to three different places to make sure it got to me – about my first book, which he said he read "with interest." He then went on:

> What do you see as the theme of the story? Does it have an explicit theme (?), are there a multiplicity of themes that you weave (?), or do you see it simply as a slice of life revolving around the unfortunate circumstances in these children's lives? Perhaps I am naïve or just an imperceptive reader, but I sure would appreciate your input here.

By golly, he read the book! At the end he even says he enjoyed it. But that isn't enough; he has to know the "theme." Just like those earnest interviewers who ask, "But what are you really trying to say?" Or worse, the ones who say, "Of course this is a novel about the breakup of the Soviet Union." Ho-ho, and you thought it was a middle-aged love story.

With readers like these – who can't simply listen, who have to be told – one sometimes thinks, in darker moments, that the writer is "well out of it."

A few years ago I became friends with a woman who had been a highly distinguished and successful architect, and a sculptor rather less successfully, as most of her sculptures were done in foam rubber which has a tendency to wither, sag, perish, and, finally, disintegrate. In her late forties, she suddenly gave the whole thing up – everything. "I am going to do nothing for the rest of my life," she told me, "and I am going to live to be very, very old. I hope I have enough money to do nothing." (Which, as she was an oil heiress, was a bit of an understatement.) This particularly appealed to me because I happened to be going through one of those periods – which we all go through now and again – when it seems that moral and literary integrity could only be maintained by absolute silence. One day I suggested that instead of leaving her jewelry lying about (she had an aversion to safes), she should put it in one of those hollowed-out books. And suddenly hollowed-out books seemed the solution to everything. We would have an entire library of empty books. How many? Why not 365 – one for each day of the year? But they would have to be proper bound books, with dust jackets, with titles – with blurbs. So, while she set to work on estimates for binding and shelving, paper and printing and artwork for the jackets, I set to work on the blurbs. This was my first one:

BACKWARDS by Julian Gloag

Fifteen billion years ago, time, light, sound were nonexistent, absorbed in a black hole of infinitely compressed and undifferentiated matter. When the perfect order of this stasis blew apart, time, space, and light began – and raced out to disorder. This soundless explosion was the creator of the expanding universes: the Creation. Creation is the creator – just as life is the liver.

But eventually the outward movement will gradually cease until it stops altogether – the expansive force will have reached the limit of its energy. In that singular instant, time will have stopped. Already what we see at a great distance is billions of years in the past, and that past views us (if it has telescopes strong enough) as not having yet begun to exist. But at *that* moment – at the uttermost limit of unraveling – matter will begin to be knit back up again, the past will retreat toward us with increasing speed to its original order, time will move backwards to ultimate timelessness once more. Heaven is not what we move forward to, but what we go back to.

In that great retraction when time changes direction, future will become past and backwards forwards. We will step out of our coffins or be reconstituted from ashes, our wrinkles will be smoothed and every day our step will become lighter, into our assholes we will ingest the muck of the world and from our mouths produce food, we will wake exhausted at night but will gather strength as the day winds back to the springing dawn, we will say not "all things must die" but "all things must be born"; our infirmities will be made whole and we will return to an innocent and earlier state of nature – until we slip easily at last into our mother's womb.

In this magisterial new novel (his 365th), Julian Gloag portrays a world, not as it is or as we have known it, but as, inexorably, it will be. *Backwards*, as its name implies, may present certain initial difficulties to the reader – for example, the fact that it transports us to a time before the book was written means that all the pages are blank. Nevertheless, from last to first, few will disagree that this is a work of monumental scope and brilliant originality. Like some of his other notable novels – such as *Silence, Erasures, Whiteness Is All – Backwards* moves us triumphantly into a territory of wonder and nullity that Julian Gloag has long marked out as his own.

Well, for one reason and another, the project came to nothing – a suitable denouement in the circumstances. But the main reason was that, having written a few of these blurbs, I began to have an overwhelming urge to put something inside those hollow books. Even if it was only hay for the horse.

What am I saying? That you can't keep a good novelist down? Not exactly – because of course you can, it's being done all the time.

Am I saying that nobody is listening at all? Not that either. But just as television makes us blind, so bad books drive out good books and make us deaf – blind and deaf with boredom. Years and years ago, when I was but a lad, my psychiatrist said to me, "But, Julian, life *is* boring." Nonsense, I don't believe a word of it – I didn't then and I don't now. I don't believe, in their heart of hearts, anybody wants to be bored. And, if they listen to *us,* they won't be. The problem is to reach them. The intelligence of the age and the sensibility of our civilization is seriously endangered by the ignorant, the greedy, and the power-mad, who treat the writer with scorn and the reader as a donkey. But greed, ignorance, and megalomania have always had to be fought, and never more so than now. It is, now, peculiarly important to keep writing. And *we* have one advantage: *we* know, *we* believe that there are millions of people out there who, though waiting with the patience of the horse maybe, are certainly not donkeys.

In the end, if we cannot by hook or by crook get through to this public readership, we can always turn to – and teach and amuse – that smaller audience, our own children: innocent listeners eager to be enthralled.

MICHAEL DENNIS BROWNE

Failure

[SPLIT ROCK ARTS PROGRAM]

In 1992 a fourth collection of my poems was published. I worked hard on that book; one poem in particular, about my mother, took me more than three years to finish. I think I managed to get into that poem a good deal of the intense confusion and grief I felt in the months following her death, and it is likely one of the best things I have written. The poem is a failure. There are two or three other poems in the collection of which I might say, as I say of the poem about my mother: "I can't do that very often." The book that contains these poems is a failure.

Why should I say that? I am hardly sorry for myself. Nor am I boasting of failure. I remember a teacher in France, long ago, who used to come into the staff room at the Lycée de Garçons and declare, with a broad smile on his face: "Je suis modeste et je ne le cache pas!" (I am modest and I do not hide the fact.) Failure is something I expect and accept as a writer, and today I want to try to say what I mean by calling one of my better poems, and my new book, a failure. Along the way I'll pass on the thoughts of some other writers that I have found helpful on this subject.

I am borrowing, of course, from George Orwell. In his essay "Why I Write," Orwell says:

> I will only say that of late years I have tried to write less picturesquely and more exactly. In any case I find that by the time you have perfected any style of writing, you have always outgrown it. *Animal Farm* was the first book in which I tried, with full consciousness of what I was doing, to fuse political purpose and artistic purpose into one whole. I have not written a novel for seven years, but I hope to write another fairly soon. It is bound to be a failure, every book is a failure, but I know with some clarity what kind of book I want to write.

I like how Orwell tosses that phrase down on the page between a couple of commas – ",every book is a failure," – for him it's a given, and moves right on to the next thought.

Let's look at his statement for a moment. Most of us would not think of *Animal Farm,* for example, as a failure – I certainly don't. But if it is, at least in some measure, could the "full consciousness" Orwell speaks of have been part of the problem? Might the whole thing have been too willed, too clearly illustrative of a prior concept, rather than imagined? Or, in general terms, might every book have to seem a failure to the writer so that the next one becomes necessary? Is there a way in which we can see acknowledgment of a book's "failure" not as something that quenches the imagination, that robs the writer of confidence for future work, but rather as an incentive to – forgive the hearty phrases – do it better, to get it right, next time?

The "it" is constantly changing, of course, which is part of the problem, part of the challenge. Orwell says that a style reaches perfection always too late, which may mean that some new content has begun to suggest itself for which a fresh style is required ("Form is never more than an extension of content"). For a poet, it can also be that a new way of using language, some rhythmical surge of phrases or pulsing of syntax, is proposing itself independent of any foreseeable content. In either case, while one is still coming into full articulation of the original subject, as the "full consciousness" is earnestly at work on the topic at hand, the good old anarchic unconscious is whispering of new horizons and subverting the whole enterprise. Eliot puts it this way:

> . . . and every attempt
> Is a wholly new start, and a different kind of failure
> Because one has only learnt to get the better of words
> For the thing one no longer has to say, or the way in which
> One is no longer disposed to say it.

Different occasions require different responses from us as writers, and as new subjects occur to us, or are thrust upon us, we need real flexibility of response if we are to catch them with the palpable forms of poems. How do we stay faithful to what we had thought we wanted to write about while incorporating newly generated ideas, or forms, which may or may

not be organic to that subject matter? Such tension of decisions is always
with the writer, and a certain formal restlessness, characteristic of many
great writers, seems appropriate through the course of an artistic lifetime.

A single lifetime isn't long enough, very obviously, to do all that is proposed internally by our own imaginations, and a feeling of failure may
consist not only in the suspicion that style and content have somehow fallen out in a particular work and begun to renege on their original vows,
but also in a feeling of incompletion. Just as we finally abandon each work
rather than complete it (to quote Valéry), so too we run out of time to
carry out all the tasks we can envision. "I'll go to my grave with a million
things unsaid," I remarked once to a student, meaning to sound matter-
of-fact rather than grandiosely mournful, and probably failing at that.
This was the same student who had written, in an end-of-term assessment: "I'm worried about what I'm avoiding in my work." The topic of
avoidance, its intimate links to failure, is a whole talk (or two) in itself.
But while it's impossible not to refer to the griefs that can be associated
with failure, my main purpose here is to rescue the word from merely dire
connotations, dust it off a little, and then return it to its place in the life of
the writer.

I don't see the sense of incompletion as something necessarily desperate but rather as something inevitable, which I need to learn to accept
and even embrace. As artists we have to acknowledge the approximate-
ness of what we can accomplish. This awareness is not going to stop me
from taking on large projects, from robing myself in some ancient naïveté
as I sit down to take on something all the sensible parts of me know (and
shriek at me) I can never manage. Foreknowledge of failure is not a lid on
our expectations. I very much like the way Eavan Boland, a contemporary Irish poet, talks about this.

I always think of myself as working at a rock face. Ninety days out of ninety-five,
it's just a rock face. The other five days, there's a bit of silver, a bit of base metal in
it. I'm reasonably consistent, and the consistency is a help to me. It helps me to
stay in contact with my failure rate, and unless you have a failure rate that vastly
exceeds your success rate, you're not really in touch with what you're doing as a
poet. The danger of inspiration is that it is a theory that redirects itself towards the
idea of success rather than to the idea of consistent failure. And all poets need to
have a sane and normalized relationship with their failure rate.

These remarks (from an interview in *Sleeping with Monsters: Conversations with Scottish and Irish Women Poets*), their matter-of-factness, seem to me exactly helpful. Here's a working writer, a first-rate poet, who sees acquaintance with her own failure as a very necessary part of her own process. Once again, it's not a matter of self-pity: simply, we need to stay in dialogue with whoever inside us is able to be ruthless about the second-rate work we do and is never afraid to name it, someone who can "kill the darlings" (Faulkner's phrase) every time it becomes necessary (that will be often). We need to see the very words "success" and "failure," such hardened polarities, as a large part of the problem, and get ourselves out from under the shadow of such dualities. And the separating of what's good from what's not, in revision after revision, something every writer is familiar with, should perhaps be reinstated as an intuitive, muscular activity rather than as a primarily cerebral one, something carried out, as Boland has it, by a worker at a rock face or, to improvise a figure of my own, like a bouncer in a bar. Throw the rascals out!

Here's another quotation, one that I read in a biography of Einstein. Once again, an inner process is imaged as a physical activity. Toward the end of his life, Sir Isaac Newton wrote this:

> I do not know what I may appear to the world; but to myself I seem to have been only like a boy, playing on the sea-shore, and diverting myself, in now and then finding a smoother pebble or prettier shell than ordinary, whilst the great ocean of truth lay all undiscovered before me.

While there's something rueful about this admission, I suspect that even if Newton had guessed early on in his inventive life that it would come down to this, he would not have "ceased from exploring."

Should we allow our conviction of our own limitations to harden into a sense of inferiority and so hold back our curiosity? What can we do to counter the persistent inner voice, the one that never tires of telling us that we won't make it but that others will, that whispers to us that our own pretensions are laughable? One thing we might do is to image alternative mental states, conjure inner landscapes where creation typically takes place. Patients suffering from certain types of cancer can be taught to do this, sometimes with startling results. One image I have found especially helpful comes from the Spanish writer José Ortega y Gasset.

So many things fail to interest us, simply because they don't find in us enough surfaces on which to live, and what we have to do then is increase the number of
planes in our mind so that a much larger number of themes can find a place in it at
the same time.

I'll give you my own simple visualization of Ortega y Gasset's statement.
Imagine a flock of several hundred birds looking, toward the end of day,
for a place to spend the night. They fly right on past the tree that has
only a branch or two and a mere couple of dozen twigs – not enough for
them, not nearly enough surfaces. When they find a tree that has many
branches, multiple twigs, that's where they land, and settle in. In my
own experience, there are plenty of poems I have failed to write, or to
complete, because I wasn't able to provide enough surfaces for landing,
and so some powerful visions passed me by. An image is, says Pound, a
"visual chord," is "that which presents an intellectual and emotional
complex in an instant of time," and the imagination needs to be constantly renewing itself, putting forth new surfaces, if it is to be host to
new subjects and new language that constantly propose themselves to us.
I feel challenged by this image, try to keep it in mind and draw upon it
rather than sink into a stupor of imageless despair. As I get older, I find
myself more excited than ever by the issues I might be able to write
about, and at the same time properly humbled by my abilities to make
poetry of them. I need to work at staying open, becoming yet more open,
just as I need to keep my body flexible, the spine supple, as it ages. The
work of providing those internal surfaces also requires a toughness, requires that we be prepared to slough off old surfaces, tired habits, so that
we can stay alert for the arrival, at any time, of possibly astonishing words
and ideas.

The very idea of success, which Eavan Boland mentioned, can be poi-
soning. What is success for a poet? Not so long ago I read an interview
with a well-known poet in which he said that a certain critic had called
him one of the five or six "best" poets writing in America today. He
seemed to be approving of this statement. I have also heard a visiting
poet, a fine writer and teacher, say in front of my students that another
certain critic called him the "best" poet writing in America today. He
passed off the remark, but why did he bring it up? Against such self-
shoring notions I would set the melancholy resonance of Leonardo's

"Dimmi se mai fu fatto qualche cosa?" (Tell me if anything was ever done?), said as he was pouring water over a skull he planned to draw, or Eliot's reply to a friend who asked him, as they were crossing a London street one day: "Tom, do you know you're good?" "No," said Eliot, "do you?"

I would also set against them these words of Virginia Woolf, talking of Shakespeare's imagined sister, she who died without having written a word:

> I am talking of the common life which is the real life and not of the little separate lives which we live as individuals . . . if we have the habit of freedom and the courage to write exactly what we think; if we escape a little from the common sitting-room and see human beings not always in their relation to each other but in relation to reality . . . then the opportunity will come and the dead poet who was Shakespeare's sister will put on the body which she has so often laid down. . . . I maintain that she would come if we worked for her, and that so to work, even in poverty and obscurity, is worth while.

Here again is the idea of work, the rock face, the persistent exploring – the "real work," as Gary Snyder calls it. The vanity of the idea of success, and the corresponding polarity of failure, too often sets us, fellow artists, fellow human beings, against each other; the result is that we expend our energies in senseless competitiveness, thinking ourselves failures as we see others winning awards, prizes, critical acknowledgment. I myself am scarcely immune to these kinds of envies and depressions. What I try to do is to let them rise up, in all their unreality, have their vain say, and then let them go; I try to clear myself, get myself back to the reality of the work I have to do, which involves reality itself. That is where my obligation lies; that is where I am aimed.

The title of the book I am working on now, *In the Carpenter's House*, came to me one day as I was sweeping the floor of a small building in northern Minnesota. It stands a few yards from the main cabin on our land and it's a beautifully built structure: post and beam, wooden dowels, oak beams, pine paneling – and the floor is plywood. Still plywood, six years after the building went up. This is the "studio" where I do my work when we are in the woods, where friends stay when they come to visit. What will it take to put the floor in, the final floor of fir or oak? More money than I can presently come up with. A composer friend of mine, John Foley, S.J., stayed in the studio some years ago, just after it went up, while we were working on a piece together; and as I was sweeping the floor, all this time later, I was saying to him, in my mind: "See, John, the floor is still plywood, just as it was when you were first up here five years ago. It still isn't finished." And suddenly this provisional floor seemed to me emblematic of so much in my own writing and in my own life – it might never be finished, never be "final." The carpenter's own house is often, even notoriously, in that kind of shape – permanently unfinished – while the carpenter works at completing other people's houses. And I found this image not only liberating about a number of things in my life but also, instantly, a strong contender as the subject of a cycle of poems I would write that would then be set to music by John! I have been working at this cycle for some time now, inflamed with a sense of its possibilities, but I have a long way to go. I may get it done, and again I may not. "Ars longa, vita brevis," says the ancient poet. "The life so short, the craft so long to learn," says another. "And so it goes," says a certain contemporary writer of fiction.

You can expect too little from your own work in its relation to how you live your life. You can also dangerously expect it to substitute for the ongoing work of maintaining real relationships; an account of the toll that an excessive focus on writing can take on the quality of your living would have to be a long chapter in a book about writers and failure. You can expect too much of your writing, and once again there's a tension of decisions here that the writer must live with. Let me tell you a story both for and against a remark by D. H. Lawrence that I've always found helpful: "One sheds one's sickness in books." This suggests the therapeutic function of writing – that you can heal yourself, as an artist, by becoming conscious of something that would otherwise fester in the unconscious, stirring up all manner of unclearly motivated and bizarre behavior. I think there's a great deal of truth in this; it is not the whole story, however, and I'll show you what I mean with an illustration from my own psychological life.

In 1976 I finished a long poem called *Sun Exercises*, which was an extended elegy for my father (who died suddenly in 1960, when I was nineteen). It was an elaborate piece that combined some very direct and heartfelt mourning with some pretty indigestible references to both hatha-yoga and Egyptian mythology. Like the elegy for my mother in my most recent book, it too is a failure – though on a rather grander scale, perhaps! But at the time I was rather pleased with the poem, and when it was published as a book, in a beautiful small edition by a local press, with fascinating illustrations, I felt quite good indeed about it. A month or two after its publication, and after I had given a number of readings in which I read the poem in its entirety (it took about half an hour), I had a dream in which my father was dying in a small motel somewhere up on the north shore of Lake Superior. My father began to vomit, and out of his mouth came long rolls of white material on which there were many small, dark markings. It went on and on for hours, this flowing vomiting. The dream made a powerful impression on me and brought with it a huge effect of sadness that I did not quite understand. A few days later I realized that what my father had been vomiting up in the dream was the long, recently published poem in which I imagined I had shed the sickness of sixteen years of mourning for him, shed it with a certain amount of public and "poetry biz" attention, leading myself to believe that the grief at his death, so long subverting my joy, was past, and I could get on with my life. My interpretation – and it remains only that – was that the dream was compensating for a considerable smugness (and relief) in my conscious thinking; it was reminding me that though one can "shed one's sickness in books," the matter is never quite as simple as that, and that even after sixteen years of a certain kind of grieving, I could not bring it to closure with such apparent finality. The dream was showing me that the grieving would never be done; my father was shedding the sickness of my over-simplified notion. The corrective effect of the nightmarish dream image has stayed with me and continues to teach me that I have no choice but to stay in dialogue with a number of obsessions, of which the death of the father is one. "Failure" comes in thinking that the poem has settled the topic once and for all, or in the expectation that the topic itself will ever be quite done with. In his poem "For Sheridan," Robert Lowell writes:

> Past fifty, we learn with surprise and a sense
> of suicidal absolution
> that what we intended and failed
> could never have happened –
> and must be done better.

In other words – and it's a beautifully expressed paradox – what we have in mind to do early on as poets is both misguided and essential. What we think we need to tackle is always different from our early notions of it (we will fail if we attempt to flesh out the synopsis in extreme detail) and yet our instincts are in general accurate. If a poem itself is "best when generally not perfectly understood" (Coleridge), then perhaps we need to bring a similar latitude of expectation to our own writing lives and learn to be less rigid, relax the parameters of both what the task seems to us to be and what our ambitions for ourselves ("the idea of success") asks of us. Might that help us to do things "better"? One way to proceed is to become more philosophical, precisely as Lowell is being, and to live with the tensions of the paradox as he states it in the poem. If we can come to the realization that, as Tadeusz Rozewicz says of his poetry, "it has many tasks/to which it will never do justice," then we might possibly go about the work of poetry less dependent on recognition of our worth from external sources, more aware of ourselves as permanently apprenticed to the exploration of consciousness, to what another contemporary Polish poet, Czeslaw Milosz, calls "the passionate pursuit of reality."

Part of the problem, then, is seeing failure itself as a problem that drags us down rather than as a "losing of the scent" (one of the original meanings of the word) that one can, with patience and with persistence, resume. In his book *Care of the Soul*, Thomas Moore, a psychotherapist, sees failure as "a source of potential soul." He sees failing at something as usefully antidotal to overly high expectations; when ambition and ideas of perfection are tempered by failure, he says, something is incarnated in us that is specifically human, whereas "perfection belongs to an imaginary world." He goes on to say:

> Ordinary failures in work are an inevitable part of the descent of the spirit into human limitation. Failure is a mystery, not a problem. Of course this means not that we should try to fail, or take masochistic delight in mistakes, but that we should see the mystery of incarnation at play whenever our work doesn't measure up to our expectations. If we could understand the feelings of inferiority and humbling occasioned by failure as meaningful in their own right, then we might incorporate failure into our work so that it doesn't literally devastate us.

Let me lay another quotation right alongside this one. It comes from Boris Pasternak, from a memoir:

I do not like my style up to 1940.... I am not worried about the loss of imperfect and faulty works. But neither was I ever sorry for the loss of successful works, though for quite a different reason. In life it is more necessary to lose than to gain. A seed will only germinate if it dies. One has to live without getting tired, one must look forward and feed on one's living reserves, which oblivion no less than memory produces.

These remarks hearten me, and neither is far in essence from those of George Orwell or Eavan Boland or Isaac Newton or Virginia Woolf or José Ortega y Gasset. There's a consensus that the job is far larger than the worker. We are committed to trying to bring something to life whose measure not one of us can take in, even in a long lifetime. This should not stop us.

The ambition needs to be grounded, however, for all its possibly wild energy, in the revelation of what lies about us. When Emily Dickinson says "Nature is a Haunted House – but Art – A House that tries to be haunted," she brilliantly suggests not only the tantalizing polarities of the world we live in but also the necessity of our commitment to it as artists, if our expressiveness is to be faithful to the experience we have been born into. I'll take one last example out of my own life. When our first child was born eight years ago – a son, Peter – I was so wonderstruck by the event, and by the early months of his life, that I found myself ashamed of language itself – it seemed such a crude system of signs, such a weak vehicle to convey the complex of emotions I was going through. In the second half of a poem I wrote at this time, "To Show Peter the World," I talk first about this sense of the inadequacy of language and then come to a realization about what I must do:

> There are days, child, I have woken
> ashamed of the names, wanting
> for your entering, fresher ones
> for what you will come to know,
> and what I must learn to do, all
> over again, is trust the necessity,
> the endlessness, the grace of our naming,
> which is human, which is what we do,
> and sound again around lips and teeth and tongue,
> and roll again down bones and veins

familiar syllables, yes, the usual ones,
until they assume the unknown again,
until no name's familiar, and learn

not only to wander with you
the present borders of our naming
but to be there to watch and listen
as you begin going on beyond,
making *your* names for the things, as
Peter shows Peter the world, this place
into which we have only brought you,
and in which we must leave you.

I have not talked about many of the darkest aspects of failure, which are very real, and can lead to a paralysis – "the apple unbitten in the palm," as Philip Larkin has called it – that is living death for the writer. Certain kinds of failures can be little deaths, in which we can almost feel the cells crumbling. These deaths can accumulate until the whole system is poisoned. What I have wanted to get across is that we need to learn to live with failure and, in a sense, to die to the idea of it by incorporating it, even embracing it – I think of the image "our sister the death of the body" of Francis of Assisi. If we are aimed toward reality, if we are apprenticed to depicting it, naturally we will "fail," daily. But we can do better than live in the shadow of such dualities as success and failure. The most useful work each one of us can do as writers at any level of experience is to become, as Charlotte Joko Beck says in her book *Everyday Zen*, a "bigger container" of whatever reality is, more ready to make use of what comes into us, in all its bewildering possibilities, so that we can be those on whom, to quote Henry James's gloriously unreasonable formulation, "nothing is lost." It is an old idea that the end is the journey itself, and that in the experiencing and accepting and embracing of failure we become most fully human. Through daily personal and artistic discipline we can work to be more receptive, even if we often come to realize that the maps we have made are not the territory, that our persistent examining leads us to the conviction that, as Auden says, the truth is a silence toward which words can only point. We can see this as a pathology, a problem, or as a mystery, one to live as fully as possible.

I'll end with two quotations, and save the others for another day. The first is by Olga Broumas, from a short piece called *Some Notes on Struggle and Joy:*

> I imagine the infinite because it gives my soul pleasure, because imagining the infinite is the vocation of the soul and it, like minds and bodies, needs exercise, needs meaningful work. To imagine the possible in its infinity makes me want to fulfill it.

It is another old idea that the soul has forgotten its infinite capacities while in the body, and that the kinds of joy it is equipped for are not those the world is inclined to give. You cannot expect to get back from the world any external reward ("success") commensurate with the devotion, craft, time, soul you have put into your work. The joy lies, finally, elsewhere.

Let me end with an entire poem by the apparently successful William Butler Yeats, written in 1913, the year preceding the so-called Great War, "the war to end all wars."

TO A FRIEND WHOSE WORK
HAS COME TO NOTHING

Now all the truth is out,
Be secret and take defeat
From any brazen throat,
For how can you compete,
Being honour bred, with one
Who, were it proved he lies,
Were neither shamed in his own
Nor in his neighbours' eyes?
Bred to a harder thing
Than Triumph, turn away
And like a laughing string
Whereon mad fingers play
Amid a place of stone,
Be secret and exult,
Because of all things known
That is most difficult.

WILLIAM KITTREDGE

Doing Good Work Together

[IN THE THOREAU TRADITION]

Plot in fiction helps us overcome the anxiety caused by the loss of the "sacred masterplot" that organizes and explains the world. Our lives are ceaselessly intertwined with narrative, with the stories that we tell or hear told, those that we dream or imagine or would like to tell, all of which are reworked in that story of our own lives that we narrate to ourselves in an episodic, somewhat semiconscious, but virtually uninterrupted monologue. We live immersed in narrative...
– *Reading for the Plot*, Peter Brooks

As they are told and retold, stories have the function of wrestling with the ultimately inexplicable chaos of reality around us. They give it form, and in shaping and reshaping the form, they help us gain control over it.
– Interview with Alan Jabbour of the National Folklife Center

The poet C. K. Williams came to Missoula some years ago and spoke of "narrative dysfunction" as a prime part of mental illness in our time. Many of us, he said, lose track of the story of ourselves, the story that tells us who we are supposed to be and how we are supposed to act.

It isn't any fun, and it doesn't just happen to people; it happens to entire societies. Stories are places to live, inside the imagination. We know a lot of them, and we're in trouble when we don't know which one is ours. Or when the one we inhabit doesn't work anymore and we stick with it anyway.

We live in stories. What we are is stories. We do things because of what is called character, and our character is formed by the stories we learn to live in. Late in the night we listen to our own breathing in the dark and rework our stories. We do it again the next morning, and all day long, before the looking glass of ourselves, reinventing reasons for our lives. Other than such storytelling there is no reason to things.

Aristotle talks of "recognitions," which can be thought of as moments of insight or flashes of understanding in which we see through to coherencies in the world. We are all continually seeking after such experiences. It's the most commonplace thing human beings do, after breathing. We are like detectives, each of us trying to make sense and define what we take to be the right life. It is the primary, most incessant business of our lives.

We figure and find stories, which can be thought of as maps or paradigms in which we see our purposes defined. Then the world drifts and our maps don't work anymore, our paradigms and stories fail, and we have to reinvent our understandings and our reasons for doing things. Useful stories, I think, are radical in that they help us see freshly. They are like mirrors in which we see ourselves reflected. That's what stories are for, to help us see for ourselves as we go about the continual business of reimagining ourselves.

If we ignore the changing world and stick to some story too long, we are likely to find ourselves in a great wreck. It's happening all over the American West, right now, as so many of our neighbors attempt to live out rules derived from old models of society that simply reconfirm their prejudices.

They get to see what they want to see. Which is some consolation. But it is not consolation we need. We need direction.

The interior West is no longer a faraway land. Our great emptiness is filling with people, and we are experiencing a time of profound transition that can be thought of as the second colonization. Many people here are being reduced to the tourist business, in which locals feature as servants, hunting guides and motel maids, or local color. People want to enclose our lives in theirs, as decor.

The Native American people were living coherent lives, at one with their circumstances, when our people displaced them, leaving them mostly disenfranchised and cut off from possibility in our society. Their reservations are like little beleaguered nations battling to survive within our larger one as we continue wrecking the traditional resources of their cultures. The result, for them, is anomie, nothing to hang on to, powerlessness. We are shamed and look away, and do little to help.

So it is deeply ironic that the Native Americans are being joined in their disenfranchisement by loggers and miners and ranchers, and by the towns that depend on them. Our ancestors came to the West and made homes for themselves where they could live independent lives. Because of their sacrifices, we in the dominant society think we own the West; we think they earned it for us. But, as we know, nobody owns anything absolutely, except their sense of who they are.

One Sunday, while living in the heart of the French Quarter of New Orleans, Annick and I were out walking in the rain when we realized we were hearing the echoes of someone singing. It was a vivid unaccompanied voice in the narrow street, maybe three blocks away when I first heard her—a black woman with her eyes closed and face open to the utmost as her voice rose and fell to "Glory, Glory, Hallelujah."

She shone in the gray light. I almost couldn't look, and wondered if she cared what anybody thought as I dropped two folded dollars into the coffee can at her feet. She didn't look at me at all.

Semitropical plants were draped along the lacy ironwork balconies above the broken sidewalk, nature in a place where everything was carpentered. My shuttered door was one in a wall of shuttered doors that stretched on toward Bourbon Street, each painted thick, deep green. The light seemed to rebound from the walls, illuminating the wet bricks.

I can still hear that woman. Her life looked to be endlessly more difficult than mine. Her courage and passion were evident in her singing even if it was a street-shuck for money, and I envied her. I felt like weeping for myself, and I was afraid of it, like something in my body might break.

There I was, living near some of the best eating and drinking and music in the world, in a place where I never heard so many people—black, white, Creole, Cajun—laughing so much of the time, and I was awash with sadness.

Maybe it was because I had never lived so close to so much violence, which was the other side of things. During Mardi Gras, on Rampart Street, a little more than three blocks from our door, some lost tourist was shot every night, killed and robbed, mainly for drug money. Every week or so there was a schoolyard killing, a kid assassinating another kid with a handgun, settling scores.

The perpetrators in these crimes were most often young men from the so-called projects, publicly owned housing for the poor. Those young men were alienated and angry because they saw correctly that their situation in society was hopeless – they were essentially uneducated, their schools were war zones, and their chances of finding jobs, much less meaningful and respected work, were nil. A friend who grew up in New Orleans said, "They've got no place to go. There's no ladder up, no ladder out. They're left with nothing but selfishness. It's the second lesson you learn on the streets." The first lesson, according to my friend, is that nothing, nobody, is bulletproof.

It might be useful for us in the West to consider the ways in which the projects in New Orleans, in their capacity to generate hopelessness, are much like so many of our failing towns and our Indian reservations. It might be instructive to consider the rage that is generated by such disenfranchisement, and think of the ways it looks when it gets to the streets of our cities. It might be instructive to look closely at the events that led to rioting in Los Angeles in 1992.

It starts with broken promises. In the West, people came here thinking they had been promised something – at least freedom and opportunity, and the possibility of inventing a new, fruitful life. That was the official mythology. When that story didn't come true, the results were alienation and anomie, just like in the New Orleans projects, just like in South Central Los Angeles.

When people are excluded from what their society has defined for them as the main rewards of life, when they sense that they are absolutely out of the loop, as a lot of Americans do in the rural outback and the deep heartlands of the cities, they sometimes turn to heedless anger.

A lot of people on our streets are staring back at us, the enfranchised, with hatred that we all know to be at least partly justifiable. Some among them, we can see, might kill us for our selfishness. Fewer and fewer of them are willing to stand singing in the rain, waiting for a few dollars to accumulate in the tin can at their feet.

Many of us live with a sense that there is something deeply and fundamentally wrong in our society. Many of us feel our culture has lost track of the reasons why one thing is more significant than another. We are fearful and driven to forget the most basic generosities. We anesthetize ourselves with selfishness. It's not, we say, our fault.

Many of us live insulated, as I do much of the time. In New Orleans I liked to walk down a couple of blocks to the Bombay Club and disassociate my sensibilities with one and then another huge, perfect martini. In Las Vegas I like to stay at the brilliantly named Mirage, amid those orchids and white tigers. What I don't like to do is walk the streets and look the other side of my society in the eye.

I want to think I deserve what I get. I don't want to consider how vastly I am overrewarded. I don't want to consider the injustices around me. I don't want any encounters with the disenfranchised. I want to say it is not my fault.

But it is: it's mine, and ours. We'd better figure out ways to spread some equity around if we want to go on living in a society that is at least semifunctional. It's a fundamental responsibility to ourselves.

We inhabit a complex culture that is intimately connected to societies all over the world, vividly wealthy while increasingly polarized between rich and poor, increasingly multiethnic and multiracial, predominantly urban, sexually ambiguous, ironic, self-reflexive, drug-crazed, dangerous, and resounding with discordant energies; a selfish, inhumane society without a coherent myth to inhabit; a society coming unglued; a democracy that is failing. Its citizens do not believe in it anymore: they don't vote, they withdraw from the processes of governing themselves. On C-SPAN, all day long, you will see the other end of that same society, privileged long-faced citizens trying to figure out what to do about our troubles without forgoing their privileges. You will see a society without much idea of how to proceed.

I want to inhabit a story in which the animals all lie down with one another, everybody satisfied, children playing on sandy beaches by a stream, in the warm shade of the willows, the flash of salmon in the pools. Children of your own as you see them. How do we understand our kingdom?

It is easy to see that the world is luminous with significances. We want them to be part of the story of our life, the most important characters after ourselves. We yearn to live in a coherent place we can name, where we can feel safe. We want that place to exist like a friend, somebody we can know. What we need most urgently, both in the West and all over America, is a fresh dream of who we are that will tell us how we should act, a set of stories to reassure us in our sense that we deserve to be loved. We want the story of our society to have a sensible plot. We want it to go some-where; we want it to mean something.

We must define some stories about taking care of what we've got, which is to say *life* and *our lives*. They will be stories in which our home is sacred, stories about making use of the place where we live without ruin-ing it, stories that tell us to stay humane amid our confusions.

We must define a story that encourages us to understand that the liv-ing world cannot be replicated. We hear pipe dreams about cities in space, but it is clearly impossible to replicate the infinite complexities of the world in which we have evolved. Wreck it, and we will have lost our-selves, and that is craziness. We are animals evolved to live in the inter-penetrating energies and subjectivities of all the life there is, which coats the rock of earth like moss. We cannot live without connection, both psy-chic and physical. We begin to die of pointlessness when we are isolated, even if some of us can hang on for a long while connected to nothing be-yond our imaginations.

We need to inhabit stories that encourage us to pay close attention. We need stories that will encourage us toward acts of the imagination that in turn will drive us to the arts of empathy, for each other and for the world. We need stories that will encourage us to understand that we are part of everything, that the world exists under our skins, and that destroying it is a way of killing ourselves. We need stories that will drive us to care for one another and for the world. We need stories that will drive us to take action.

We need stories that tell us reasons why taking care, why compassion and the humane treatment of our fellows is more important – and inter-esting – than feathering our own nests as we go on accumulating property and power. Our lilacs bloom, and buzz with honeybees and humming-birds. We can still find ways to live in some approximation of home-child heaven. There is no single, simple story that will define paradise for us and there never will be. As we know, the world will not stand still: ener-gies and processes are what is actual; complexity is actual.

On summer mornings I can walk down Higgins Avenue to the Farmer's Market by the old Great Northern Depot in Missoula and buy baby carrots and white daisies, zinnias, snow peas, new corn, gladioli, irises, and chard. In my simpleminded way I love the old men selling long-stemmed roses, and the hippie mothers who are becoming farm wives. I try to imagine their secrets.

When I buy, I like to deal with the Hmong, refugees from the highlands of Laos. They have been in Montana since the end of hostilities in Vietnam. They were relocated courtesy of the CIA, their cohorts in the narcotics trade – at least that's the story we were told. I wonder if their old people are crazy with grief for lost villages. Maybe they are, or maybe they were glad to escape.

On the wall above the place where I write there is a bedspread embroidered by a Hmong woman: imaginary animals on a field of tropical green, a royal red elephant with black ears, a turtle with a yellow and blue and red checkered shell, a black rabbit, an orange monkey on a branch, a parrot, a peacock, and a green prehistoric creature with white horns. It is the work of a woman transported a long way from her homeland, who stayed tough enough to dream up another story. It gives me heart.

MARY CLEARMAN BLEW

The Art of Memoir

[YELLOW BAY WRITERS' WORKSHOP]

One of the oldest and loveliest of quilt patterns is the Double Wedding Ring, in which bands of colors lock and interlock in endless circles. If you want to make a Double Wedding Ring quilt, be a saver of fabric. Treasure the smallest scraps, from the maternity dress you have just sewn for your oldest daughter or the Halloween costume you cobbled together for your youngest, from the unfaded inside hems of worn-out clothing or the cotton left over from other quilts. Keep a pair of sharp scissors on hand, and also a pattern, which I like to cut from fine sandpaper, and which will be about an inch wide by two inches long and slightly flared, like a flower petal that has been rounded off at both ends. Whenever you have a scrap of fabric, lay out your pattern on it and snip out a few more blocks.

Save your blocks in a three-pound coffee can. When the can is full, empty the blocks out on the floor and arrange them in the shape of rainbow arcs with a juxtaposition of colors and textures that pleases you. Seven pieces to an arc, seventy-two arcs to a quilt. You can sew the blocks together on a sewing machine, but I like the spell cast by hand sewing. I use a #11 needle, which is an inch-long sliver of steel with an eye so fine that it will barely take the quilter's thread, which measures time by growing infinitesimally shorter with each dip and draw of the needle, and I wear the hundred-year-old thimble of a woman named Amelia Bunn on my finger.

When you have pieced your seventy-two arcs, you must choose a fabric to join your arcs, in a process that is called "setting up" the quilt. Traditionally a Double Wedding Ring quilt is set up on white, but remember that you have all colors to choose from; and while choosing one color means forgoing others, remind yourself that your coffee can of pieces will

fill again. There will be another quilt at the back of your mind while you
are piecing, quilting, and binding this one, which perhaps you will give to
one of your daughters, to trace her childhood through the pieces. Or perhaps you will give it to a friend, to speak the words the pattern spoke to
you.

For years I thought of myself as a fiction writer, even during the years in
northern Montana when I virtually stopped writing. But in 1987 I came to
a divide. My father had died, and my husband was suffering a mental
breakdown along with the progressive lung disease that eventually killed
him. I was estranged from my older children. Then I lost my job. It was
the job that mattered the most. I had a small child to support. And so I
looked for another job and found one, teaching in a small college in
Idaho, with the northern Rockies between me and the first half of my
life.

Far from home and teaching again after years in higher-ed. administration, I felt a hollowness that writing fiction seemed to do nothing to fill.
And so I started all over again, writing essays to retrieve the past – in my
case, the Montana homestead frontier with its harsh ideals for men and
women, its tests and its limitations. The conventions of fiction, its masks
and metaphors, came to seem more and more boring to me, like an un-
necessary barricade between me and the material I was writing about.
But because fiction was what I knew about, I used the techniques of fiction in these essays: plot, characterization, dialogue. What I began to discover was a form that worked for my purpose.

I would select an event out of family legend and retell it in a voice that
grew out of my own experience and perceptions. Often the events that
beckoned to me the most urgently were the ones that had been preserved
in the "secret stories" my grandmothers and my great-aunts told around
their Sunday tables after the dishes had been washed, elliptical and
pointless and mystifying, in hushed voices that dropped or stopped altogether at the approach of one of the men or an unwise question from an
eavesdropping child. Eventually I was trusted with a few of the secret
stories, myself. I remember how my aunt's voice fell and her sentences
became sparing when she told me a story about her mother, my grandmother. The story was about a time when my grandmother had lived
alone on the homestead north of Denton, Montana, for eighteen months

without seeing another woman. She had two small children and another baby on the way—her husband was away for weeks on end, trying to sell life insurance to make ends meet—and she had to carry her water in a bucket from a spring a quarter of a mile from the homestead shack, which she did at twilight, when the heat of the sun was not so oppressive. She began to hallucinate. She saw the shapes of women on the other side of the spring, shapes that looked like her dead mother and her dead sister, beckoning to her. She decided she was going crazy. She had her little children to think about. They might not be found for weeks if she broke down. And so she began to go for her water in the heat of the day, when the sun scorched her trail and bleached the color out of the grass and rocks. She never saw the beckoning shapes again.

Unlike my grandmother, I have chosen to follow the beckoning shapes. I don't understand the significance of that story for my grandmother, or why she kept it a secret except for the one time she whispered it to her younger sister in, I presume, those same stark sentences in which her sister whispered it to her niece, my aunt, the same sentences in which my aunt whispered the story just one time to me. But then, I don't fully understand why I continue to wear Amelia Bunn's thimble—it is sterling silver and engraved AB in a fine script—any more than I know what my great-grandmother looked like in life or as she appeared in the dying heat waves of that long-ago Montana twilight.

But sometimes I think I can see the turning points in the lives of dead men and women. For example, my grandmother's decision to return to schoolteaching in 1922, even though it meant breaking up her family, boarding out her oldest daughter, taking the younger children to live with her in a teacherage, leaving her husband alone on the homestead. What did that decision mean to her? I know what it means to me. Or my aunt's mowing machine accident in June of 1942, when a runaway team of sorrel horses spilled her in the path of a sickle bar that nearly cut off her foot. The disaster forced her out of the path of teaching in rural schools that she had been following and into a new life on the Olympic Peninsula. Did she understand the opportunity in the teeth of the sickle bar?

I feel an uneasy balance between writing about my grandmother and my aunt as their lives "really" were and writing about them as a projection of my own experiences. I keep reminding myself that the times when they lived are not my times. Nor do the nuances of their stories necessarily reflect my assumptions about language. And yet I am who I am because of these women and the stories they told; and, as I write about them, they live and breathe again through the umbilical tangle between character and writer.

I've been fortunate in my family's being one of storytellers and private writers who have "documented" their past. Tales, diaries, notebooks, and letters – they saved every scrap. Of course their stories were fictions as much as mine are, told over and over again and given shape and significance. Their connection to literal truth is suspect.

For my part, I struggled for a long time with the conflicting claims of the exact truth of the story and its emotional truth as I perceived it. I restrict myself to what I "know" happened: the concrete details, the objects, the history. When I speculate, I say so.

But any story depends upon its shape. In arranging the scraps that have been passed down to me, which are to be selected, which discarded? The boundaries of creative nonfiction will always be as fluid as water.

Students often ask, what can you decently write about other people? Whose permission do you have to ask? What can you decently reveal about yourself?

I can only speak for myself. I own my past and my present. Only I can decide whether or how to write about it. Also, I know that once I write about the past, I will have changed the past, in a sense set it in concrete, and I will never remember it in quite the same way. The experience itself is lost; like the old Sunday storytellers who told and retold their stories until what they remembered was the tale itself, what I will remember is what I have written.

Certainly, something personal is being sacrificed, for when I write about myself, I transform myself just as I do the past. A side-effect is that while the writing process itself can be painful, I experience a detachment from the finished essay, because I have come to exist in it as a character as separate from myself as any fictional character. I find that I can read my essays to audiences with very little emotion, although once, reading Annick Smith's essay "Homestead" to a creative writing class, I began to cry and thought I would not be able to go on. Her nonfiction character moved me in a way my own could not.

Lately I have been reading my aunt's diaries, which she kept without fail for fifty years. I feel haunted by the parallels between her life and mine. She chose, perhaps with greater self-discipline, perhaps from being closer to the source of the old punishing pressures, to stay all her life on a straight and narrow path I had been perilously near to embarking on. Her diaries reveal her unhappiness, her gradual, unwilling resignation to her lot, and finally, in her old age, her reconciliation with the lone woman she had set out to be. Which has left me with an enormous determination to resist those pressures and to try a new direction: having written my past, I will write the present and transform myself, as she did, in the interstices between fragment and pattern, through the endless interlocking connections between storyteller and story.

We'll see, we'll see. Opportunity lies in the teeth of the sickle bar.

AGHA SHAHID ALI

The True Subject: The Poetry of Faiz Ahmed Faiz

[SANTA FE WRITERS' CONFERENCE]

On April 5, 1988 – at the height of the *intifada* in the occupied territories – a "Special to the New York Times" appeared in the paper with the headline PALESTINIAN'S POEM UNNERVES ISRAELIS. The reference was to "Those Who Pass Between Fleeting Words," by Mahmoud Darwish, probably the most popular poet in the Arab world (he also takes care of cultural affairs for the executive committee of the Palestine Liberation Organization). As usual, the focus remained on the reactions of the Israelis, their "fears." Such a syntax – which hides the very significance of the information it is giving – doesn't allow the reader to become curious, to wonder about Darwish and his poetry. How many poetry editors, after reading the *Times* story, have solicited translations of the poet? Such a syntax, by keeping the focus on the Israelis, doesn't allow one to ask: So the Palestinians, those *terrorists*, have poets? And find time, in the midst of oppression, to write *poetry?* And the PLO has a department of *cultural* affairs? The *New York Times* is not interested in the culture of the Palestinians nor, really, in that of any of the Arabic-speaking peoples. Nor is much of the United States. Professors and students in the country's Master of Fine Arts writing programs have read the Israeli poet Yehuda Amichai, but who has heard of Darwish or any other Arab poet? (Some mystically inclined ones know of the nonthreatening Kahlil Gibran.) What is particularly distressing is that despite the attention paid to the Middle East, hardly any American poet has shown curiosity about non-

Israeli writers in the region (I did recently learn that W. S. Merwin is translating some Arabic poetry, including that of Darwish). Hardly any American poet has had the desire, it seems, to read between the often subversively ethnocentric lines of reports sent by American journalists in the Middle East. Why can't they see through the mystification of politics that governs those reports?

This ethnocentrism is not just visible in attitudes toward the Middle East; it is visible, quite clearly, in attitudes toward the entire Muslim world – a fact that may help explain why *The True Subject* (Princeton University Press, 1988), Naomi Lazard's excellent translation of Faiz Ahmed Faiz's poetry, has been virtually ignored. A handsome bilingual edition (the Urdu calligraphy by Ashfaq Ahmed is truly elegant), *The True Subject* is part of Princeton University Press's prestigious Lockert Library of Poetry in Translation series (Cavafy too is part of the series, as is Seferis), but just about no review has appeared. Why?

Curiosity about Faiz, actually, should have grown even before the appearance of these translations. In the September 1984 issue of *Harper's* (two months before Faiz died in Lahore), Edward Said, in his essay "The Mind of Winter: Reflections on Life in Exile," wrote:

> To see a poet in exile – as opposed to reading the poetry of exile – is to see exile's antinomies embodied and endured. Several years ago I spent some time with Faiz Ahmed Faiz, the greatest of contemporary Urdu poets. He had been exiled from his native Pakistan by Zia ul-Haq's military regime and had found a welcome of sorts in the ruins of Beirut. His closest friends were Palestinian, but I sensed that although there was an affinity of spirit between them, nothing quite matched – language, poetic convention, life history. Only once, when Eqbal Ahmad, a Pakistani friend and fellow exile, came to Beirut, did Faiz seem to overcome the estrangement written all over his face.

The three of them, late one night,

> sat in a dingy restaurant . . . and Faiz recited poems to us. After a time he and Eqbal stopped translating his verses for my benefit, but it did not matter. For what I watched required no translation: an enactment of homecoming steeped in defiance and loss, as if to say exultantly to Zia, "We are here."

Shouldn't these words of a truly distinguished literary critic, published in *Harper's,* a magazine rather difficult to ignore, have raised some curiosity? *Harper's* itself should have solicited translations of Faiz. (Another poet worth bringing to America's attention is the Iranian Said Sultanpour, who was tortured during the Shah's time and executed during Khomeini's. His body was thrown into an unmarked grave.)

When I came to the United States more than ten years ago, I found myself frustrated at discovering that no one, absolutely no one, had heard of Faiz (at that time, very few had heard even of the Turkish poet Nazim Hikmet – a friend of Faiz's and like him a winner of the Lenin Prize for Literature; some of Hikmet's poems were translated into Urdu by Faiz). To have to introduce Faiz's name, a name that is mentioned in Pakistan – to quote Naomi Shihab Nye – as often as the sun is, seemed a terrible insult. In the subcontinent we consider him a giant. As Naomi Lazard says in her introduction to *The True Subject,* "This century has given us a few great poets whose stance and influence have altered the consciousness of the world: Pablo Neruda, César Vallejo and Ernesto Cardenal in the Western hemisphere; Nazim Hikmet and Yannis Ritsos in the Middle East; and Faiz Ahmed Faiz in South Asia." Nevertheless, one fellowship-awarding committee told Naomi Lazard that it was not convinced of the literary importance of her translation project – *this* about a poet who drew as many as fifty thousand people to his readings, a poet whose work is quoted by heart by the literate and the illiterate, a poet whose lines were recited even by those who opposed him. When UNESCO was approaching various governments to nominate *the* representative writers of their countries – for the purpose of translating them into English – the then president of Pakistan, Ayub Khan, first mentioned Faiz (and Ayub Khan, I believe, had briefly jailed him). As Edward Said says elsewhere,

The crucial thing to understand about Faiz . . . is that like García Márquez he was read and listened to both by the literary élite and by the masses. His major – indeed it is unique in any language – achievement was to have created a contrapuntal rhetoric and rhythm whereby he would use classical forms *(qasida, ghazal, masnavi, qita)* and transform them before his readers rather than break from the old forms. You could hear old and new together. His purity and precision were astonishing, and you must imagine therefore a poet whose poetry combined the sensuousness of Yeats with the power of Neruda. He was, I think, one of the greatest poets of this century, and was honored as such throughout the major part of Asia and Africa.

So here was this poet whose work I had grown up reciting and hearing recited by heart, a poet whose *ghazals,* lyric poems, had been (and continue to be) sung by the leading singers of the subcontinent (including the legendary Begum Akhtar), a poet who was such a master of the *ghazal* that he transformed its every stock image and, as if by magic, brought absolutely new associations into being. (For example, the beloved – an archetypal figure in Urdu poetry – can mean friend, woman, God. Faiz not only tapped into these meanings but extended them to include the Revolution. So the reader does, to quote Said, "hear old and new together." Waiting for the Revolution can be as agonizing and intoxicating as waiting for one's lover.) And yet here was a poet who was just not known in this part of the world. So I began attempting some translations, imbibing a few of the methods Adrienne Rich and W. S. Merwin had adopted in translating Ghalib, whom Faiz often echoed, but my attempts were somewhat feeble, my results uneven.

And then, quite by chance, I came across five of Naomi Lazard's translations in *Kayak.* I was immediately struck by how good they were, and I was eager to find more of her translations. I also wanted to find out more about her. Because the world – at least of poetry – can be delightfully small, a series of coincidences led me several months later to a phone conversation with her and, shortly after that, a meeting in New York. I learned that she and Carolyn Kizer were collaborating on a joint volume of Faiz translations, that Kizer had known Faiz since the 1960s, when she met him in Pakistan, and that Lazard had met him at an international literary conference in Honolulu in 1979 – the only time, I believe, he was allowed into the country. Otherwise, the McCarran-Walter Act had kept him from these shores. On meeting him, Lazard says, she immediately knew she was in the presence of a poet of world stature, one who must be brought to the attention of her compatriots. And so the translation process began, right there at the conference. Lazard writes:

We established a procedure immediately. Faiz gave me the literal translation of a poem. I wrote it down just as he dictated it. Then the real work began. I asked him questions regarding the text. Why did he choose just that phrase, that word, that

image, that metaphor? What did it mean to him? There were cultural differences.
What was crystal clear to an Urdu-speaking reader meant nothing at all to an American. I had to know the meaning of every nuance in order to re-create the poem.

This translation process continued across continents, through the mail;
on a few occasions Lazard was able to meet Faiz during his visits to London. When Faiz died, she already had enough poems for a book; Carolyn
Kizer suggested that they abandon their collaboration and that Naomi
bring out her translations as a separate volume. And Princeton, luckily,
proved to be an enlightened press.

In choosing the title, Lazard has shown the same care that she has ex-
hibited throughout her project, engaged as she has been in what she calls
a labor of love and conviction. By way of an epigraph, she offers a "ring of
quotations regarding the true subject of poetry":

> Faiz Ahmed Faiz to Alun Lewis, Burma, circa 1943:
> "The true subject of poetry is the loss of the beloved."

> Alun Lewis, in a letter to Robert Graves
> before Lewis was killed Burma, 1944:
> "The single poetic theme of Life and Death – the question
> of what survives of the beloved."

> Robert Graves, in *The White Goddess*,
> quoting Alun Lewis, 1947:
> "The single poetic theme of Life and Death – the question
> of what survives of the beloved."

> Naomi Lazard to Faiz Ahmed Faiz, Honolulu, 1979
> (having read *The White Goddess* many years before
> and misquoting the line attributed to Alun Lewis):
> "The true subject of poetry is the loss of the beloved."

And the loss of the beloved *is* the subject of Faiz's poetry, a fact that is
quite apparent in the poems included in *The True Subject*. For example,
one of the first poems Faiz gave Lazard was "Spring Comes," the literal
version of which has the following sentence: "The book returns replete

with the heart's suffering" – the only time "the book" is mentioned in the original Urdu. After learning from Faiz that the book is a ledger in which experience is recorded, Lazard was able to give her translation its final shape by making the book, without even mentioning it, a controlling image:

> Spring comes; suddenly all those days return,
> all the youthful days that died on your lips,
> that have been waiting in Limbo, are born again
> each time the roses display themselves.
> Their scent belongs to you; it is your perfume.
> The roses are also the blood of your lovers.
> All the torments return, melancholy with the suffering of friends,
> intoxicated with embraces of moon-bodied beauties.
> All the chapters of the heart's oppression return,
> all the questions and all the answers
> between you and me.
> Spring comes, ready with all the old accounts reopened.

Thus Spring comes – but without the beloved; as a result, the heart continues to suffer oppression. The beloved has the power to end this oppression, as does the Revolution to end another kind of oppression.

In Faiz's poetry, suffering is seldom, perhaps never, private (in the sense the suffering of confessional poets is). Though deeply personal, it is almost never isolated from a sense of history and injustice. In a very famous poem, "Don't Ask Me Now, Beloved," Faiz breaks from Urdu's traditional way of looking at the beloved. Not only does he refuse to despair but, in a radical departure from convention, asks the beloved – even while acknowledging her immense importance – to accept his social commitment as more important than their love:

> Don't ask me now, Beloved, to love you as I did
> when I believed life owed its luster to your existence.
> The torments of the world meant nothing; you alone could make me suffer.
> Your beauty guaranteed the spring, ordained its enduring green.
> Your eyes were all there was of value anywhere.
> If I could have you, fate would bow before me.

None of this was real; it was all invented by desire.
The world knows how to deal out pain, apart from passion,
and manna for the heart, beyond the realm of love.
Warp and woof, the trappings of the rich are woven
by the brutish spell cast over all the ages;
human bodies numbed by filth, deformed by injuries,
cheap merchandise on sale in every street.
I must attend to this too: what can be done?
Your beauty still delights me, but what can I do?
The world knows how to deal out pain, apart from passion,
and manna for the heart, beyond the realm of love.
Don't ask from me, Beloved, love like that one long ago.

This was a revolutionary poem in Urdu, one envied by many Urdu poets who wish they had first broken from the tradition in which everything was either the beloved or nothing. Faiz did not discard the tradition: the poem clearly establishes the importance of the beloved and her beauty. But it does some plain speaking (almost like Cordelia to Lear), granting love its due but no more. Of course, that Faiz had emphasized political commitment here did not mean that he would not, in other poems, address the beloved in the traditional manner, showing how the speaker's life depended entirely on her. But then often, when he is addressing the beloved, he is also addressing a figure that, depending on the context, may very well be the Revolution – Revolution as a lost lover or a cruel lover who is refusing to return. So the subject of poetry continues to be true: the loss of the beloved. Even in "Don't Ask Me Now, Beloved," the discerning reader will notice it. For that beloved, whom he was able to love exclusively earlier, at the expense of everything else, is still beautiful, a fact that must be acknowledged even though she does not occupy the position she had before. The poet, thus, accepts his political responsibilities but with an intense awareness of the ease that has been lost. In a better world, Faiz might be saying, he would be giving his attention exclusively to the beloved.

In this poem, Faiz is of course drawing a line of demarcation between the political and the romantic. But, often, a mingling of the political and the romantic pervades his poetry. Sometimes the two, especially in the *ghazals*, are entangled in such a way that there is no point in trying to separate them: the political meaning informs the romantic and the romantic, the political. However, Faiz, a man who was jailed for his beliefs, obviously does have poems, many in fact, that are exclusively political. Three such poems appeared in *Grand Street* (Summer 1985): "Once Again the Mind," "If You Look at the City from Here," and "*You* Tell Us What to Do." Each is informed by a kind of political despair. In others, such as "The Tyrant," the despair turns into a controlled but still passionate anger ("The Tyrant" was quoted from by Salman Rushdie in *The Nation* in a piece called "Zia Unmourned." If writers from the subcontinent, especially someone as astute as Rushdie, are already quoting Lazard's translations to make their points about events in that region, then hers may very well be considered the standard translations in English). "The Tyrant" is quite direct in its strategy:

> Mine is the new religion, the new morality.
> Mine are the new laws, and a new dogma.
> From now on the priests in God's temple
> will touch their lips to the hands of idols.
> Proud men, tall as cypress trees, will bend
> to lick the dwarves' feet, and taste the clay.
>
> On this day all over earth the door of beneficent deeds is bolted.
> Every gate of prayer throughout heaven is slammed shut today.

However, Faiz has still other political poems that are not direct in this manner; instead, they are richly symbolic. And the fact that they are symbolic is sometimes in itself a political statement. Certainly, Urdu has a long enough tradition of concealing politics in symbols. In nineteenth-century Urdu poetry, the stock figure of the executioner often represented the British (a way of dodging the censors as well as the gallows: in the summer of 1857, the British had hanged almost thirty thousand people from the trees of Delhi to terrorize the population and punish it for what is often called the Mutiny). Naomi Lazard notes in her introduction that in Pakistan, under the censorship of the various dictatorships (including Zia's), it was "impossible to call things by their right names." Faiz's "When Autumn Came," for example, must "be read as a political poem." Despite – perhaps because of – its use of symbols, any reader or listener of Urdu would immediately grasp it as political. It focuses on the impossibility of calling things by their right names by creating a startling image: the "birds of dreams" lose their songs and thus become strangers (in the sense of exiles) to their songs. Lazard's effective translation comes up with a brilliant approximation:

> This is the way that autumn came to the trees:
> it stripped them down to the skin,
> left their ebony bodies naked.
> It shook out their hearts, the yellow leaves,
> scattered them over the ground.
> Anyone at all could trample them out of shape
> undisturbed by a single moan of protest.
>
> The birds that herald dreams
> were exiled from their song,
> each voice torn out of its throat.
> They dropped into the dust
> even before the hunter strung his bow.
>
> Oh, God of May, have mercy.
> Bless these withered bodies
> with the passion of your resurrection;
> make their dead veins flow with blood.
>
> Give some tree the gift of green again.
> Let one bird sing.

The last poem in the volume, "The Day Death Comes," recalls – quite appropriately – the beloved:

> No matter when death comes, or how,
> even though in the guise of the disdainful beloved who is always cold,
> there will be the same words of farewell to the heart:
> "Thank God it is finished, the night of the broken-hearted.
> Praise be to the meeting of lips, the honeyed lips I have known."

I invite readers to discover, as Naomi Lazard has, the true subject of poetry: in a voice they have not known. Then perhaps they will grasp why Faiz Ahmed Faiz's death, on November 20, 1984, was front-page news in the papers of India, Bangladesh, the Middle East, the Soviet Union, and many other countries. The leading obituary in *The Times* of London was that of Faiz. In Pakistan, his death was the main headline in all the national dailies. Messages of condolence poured in from all over the world – from, among others, Rajiv Gandhi, Yasir Arafat, Mahmoud Darwish. A wreath was placed on his body by the Soviet ambassador to Pakistan. Even Zia ul-Haq expressed "grief." But there was not a word in *The New York Times*. And none in *Newsweek*. None in *Time*. Strangely enough, there was a brief mention in *The San Francisco Chronicle*. But the rest was silence. Naomi Lazard has done brave and lonely work.

BILL BRASHLER

The Total Writer

[MIDWEST WRITERS WORKSHOP]

I want to share with you a letter that I received recently. It goes like this:

Dear Mr. Brashler,
You ruined my life. And the sad thing is, you meant well.

The year was 1983. You were a judge in the novel category for the Hopwood Awards at the University of Michigan. I was a winner. Much obliged. But you couldn't leave well enough alone. When they returned our manuscripts, the Hopwood committee included excerpts from each judge's critique.

You wrote, among other things, that my manuscript was the only entry that approaches being a professional piece of work, and the only one worth rewriting with an eye for publication.

You bastard.

That phrase has haunted me for nine years. Long after I should have pitched *The Posy Lady* in the trash and gone on to other things. I believed in that quote the way a born-again Christian believes in Christ. Every two years I'd haul out the manuscript and revise for a month or so. Horrified at how awful the previous revisions have been, I'd eventually shelve it again in despair. I staggered on like this, year after year.

Until now. Because it is finally finished. And it's not bad. Better than it was, anyway.

You're asking yourself, what will it take to make me go away?

Ha!, Ha!, Ha!, Ha!, Ha!, Ha!, Ha!

I'm sorry, where was I?

How can you put a value on a wasted life? I feel the fetid huff of mortality on the bare nape of my neck. There's no more time to fool around, not for me. I'm 32 going on 35, 34 on a good day, which may not seem so bad to you, but you haven't thrown away the most productive years of your writing life on a sophomoric piece of dreck you should have pitched the moment the Hopwood check cleared the bank.

I'm not saying, "you owe me," but then I'm not saying you don't. I'm not sure what I'm saying, frankly. Okay, we'll move on. Enclosed please find a portion of that piece of dreck referred to in the previous paragraph.

Except for the plot, the whole novel's been torn down and rebuilt several times. Including the dialogue. Among other things, you also wrote, the dialogue is uninspired. Thank you for that kindness. The dialogue stunk. However, I've spent the last eight years writing and producing award-winning humorous radio commercials and syndicated radio morning show comedy, and my dialogue's gotten a little better. If you like it any better than you did nine years ago, when you thought the book was worth rewriting with an eye toward publication, I'd appreciate a referral to your agent. Or another agent. Any agent, really. I'm not particular at this point.

Your referral can be lukewarm. Even tepid. All I need's a shot. If I don't get this monkey off my back, I'm done for. Please, I'm begging you now. Christ, I'm such a worm. For God's sake, have some compassion. Lord knows, it could be worse. I could be the son you never knew you had, come seething out of nowhere to explode your life to pieces.

As it is, I'm one of the casual leavings of your life, trying my best to deal with the good intentions that trail behind you through the long years. I know that last sentence is a little overwrought, but there's gold in there, if only we have the patience to mine it.

Cravenly kissing your shoes,

_____

P.S. Am I laying it on a little too thick? Because I can go back and rewrite, if you want. I'll drink lye, if you want. I'll nail my soft parts to a tree and run away real fast, if you think it will help.

They have passed a new law in Illinois called a "stalking law," and it seems they passed it just in time.

What the letter brings out, I think, is the longing, the ache, the angst, the passion, that is out there in people who want to be writers. People who desperately want to be writers.

I confess, I didn't always want to be a writer. In fact, writing was far from my first choice. I once met a fellow by the name of A. Scott Berg who had written a book about Maxwell Perkins, the famous editor. It was a fine book about Max and F. Scott Fitzgerald and Thomas Wolfe. Berg

said he seemed destined to write this book about Perkins and Scott Fitzgerald because when his mother was pregnant with him she was doing
nothing but reading Fitzgerald. Well, if that is true of all writers, my
mother, while she was carrying me, must have been reading the box
scores of the Detroit Tigers. For when I was born, I wanted only to be the
shortstop, or maybe the second baseman, for the Detroit Tigers. That
and that alone.

I grew up in Grand Rapids, Michigan. It is a nice place. It produced,
among other luminaries, Gerald Ford, a former president you may or may
not remember. I was brought up a Calvinist, a Dutch Calvinist. John Calvin, as some of you may know, was a no-nonsense church guy. He wrote
some pretty tough rules to live by, most of which are perfect for writers.
One of Calvin's tenets was something called "total depravity," a little
idea that says that you are really worth nothing unless you somehow at-
tain salvation. You wake up in the morning, you look in the mirror, you
are a wretched, scabies-ridden, good-for-nothing, mindless idiot – unless, as I said, something or someone redeems you.

That's great preparation for writing. Absolutely perfect. It instills in
you a sense of guilt: pure, wonderful, unadulterated guilt. You must do
something to better your existence. You must fill the page, computer
screen, whatever.

With that background, growing up in Grand Rapids, carrying the bag-
gage of John Calvin, I pursued my aim of being a ball player. In school,
however, I began reading. I discovered the power of reading, and the joy
of reading, and it was wonderful. It became a sort of an addiction. And
writing followed. I found I could read and then write just like the writer
I'd just read. It was fun. It was exciting. I also found, however, that I was
equally inspired by writers whom I was, as a Calvinist, not supposed to
read.

The Dutch Reform had a whole hit list of books that were not to be
read. *Huckleberry Finn* was in there. *The Catcher in the Rye*, and several others. Many of these were books my older brother had hidden away, which
meant I was eager to get at them. One of his hidden treasures was Henry
Miller's *Tropic of Cancer*. Have you ever gotten into that? At age twelve?
Anyway, a forbidden book that captured my attention was *Brave New
World* by Aldous Huxley. I don't know exactly why it was forbidden,
probably for some of the racy scenes in it, but I read every word.

If you remember, it is a futuristic novel. The main character is a man named Savage, and at the very end of the book, Savage commits suicide. But he doesn't commit suicide in an ordinary way. He commits the act in Huxley's extraordinary words: "Slowly, very slowly, like two unhurried compass needles, the feet turned towards the right; north, north-east, east, south-east, south, south-south-west; then paused, and, after a few seconds, turned as unhurriedly back towards the left. South-south-west, south, south-east, east . . . "

End of the book. I loved it. And I quickly shoved it back in its hiding place.

At the same time, my eighth grade was having a writing contest. Short stories. I decided to enter. Mrs. Van Kley, a woman I remember vividly and whose memory I cherish, was my teacher.

I wrote a short story about an eighth-grade kid who lived in a small Midwest town who was a blond and who didn't get along with anybody. He didn't get any respect from his parents or his siblings. One day the kid was sitting alone in his room and he looked up to discover a commotion in the street nearby. He ran out to see what the problem was.

A semitrailer truck had become wedged beneath a viaduct, and it could not get through. Traffic was backed up in either direction. There was a big crowd. What to do? The kid went up to the truck driver and said to him, "If you just take a little air out of each one of your tires, the truck will lower and go under the viaduct." "No problem," said the trucker, and he went to every tire and let some air out. The truck lowered a bit, and it eased beneath the viaduct to the crowd's cheers. The kid, of course, thought he was going to be a hero. He would be lifted from this humdrum, totally depraved life, and become someone.

But, in my short story, he didn't get the chance. The mayor of the town showed up out of nowhere, took credit for this ingenious idea, was hoisted on the shoulders of the crowd, and became the hero. And my main character, my protagonist, this unloved young boy, returned home. And what did he do? Instead of saying, "Aw, shucks," like a good Calvinist would, he committed suicide by hanging himself in his closet. And the last paragraph of my story read something like this: "Slowly, very slowly, like two unhurried compass needles, the feet turned toward the right; north, northeast . . . "

I was hoping Mrs. Van Kley had not read *Brave New World*, and I was right. I won the contest hands down, or feet up, however you want to put it. And I learned my first big lesson in writing: when in doubt, *steal*.

In the meantime, I was still playing baseball, only now I began to realize that I was not going to be big enough, fast enough, or good enough to be a member of the Detroit Tigers. So I had to fall back on my second love, which writing had become, and I went off to Calvin College and the University of Michigan. At Michigan I had the chance to hear and to meet people who wrote. Who made a difference on the page. Who inspired readers with their energy and their insight and their verve.

I remember Tom Wolfe, with his white suit and his urbane presence. I remember Kurt Vonnegut, who had just written *Cat's Cradle*, and who impressed us with his dry humor. John Barth was there, and Jerzy Kosinski. All these were fine writers and I loved them because they were passionately excited about what they were writing, what they were saying, and what they were doing. I would have given anything to have been them. I desperately wanted to be like them, to be one of them.

At the time, I was writing short stories for Michigan's Hopwood Awards. And I won. It was a wonderful honor. The Hopwoods were endowed by Avery Hopwood, the Neil Simon of his day, and they meant money. I won a thousand dollars and I wondered if I had joined, or at least made entrance, into that great fraternity of writers.

At those same awards, however, I remember what my writing mentor, John Aldridge, said to me. "Congratulations, Bill," Aldridge said. "You've probably just made as much money as you'll ever make writing." Now that's called "inspiration." And it's part of what we're all here for. We inspire each other and we beat each other down.

With my check in hand I went off to the University of Iowa Writers' Workshop, where I met Nelson Algren, Richard Yates, and William Price Fox. I became a part of what I call "the adversary method" of writing wherein everybody hates everybody else because he is afraid they are better than he is. You sold that short story to *The New Yorker?* I hate you. We were like contestants in a beauty contest where everybody hopes the other person will win Miss Congeniality and nothing more.

Nelson Algren used to read manuscripts in class – now this was Nelson Algren, author of *The Man with the Golden Arm* and other novels. Somebody who walked on the wild side. Someone I read with sheer awe – and Algren would read the short stories of a workshop student, take a dime out of his pocket, hand it to the poor kid, and say, "Kid, here's a dime. Call your father back in Grand Rapids. Tell him you want to join the heating and air conditioning business. You're never going to be a writer."

That's inspiration. But you go from there and you say, "Dammit, I'm gonna show this guy or I'm gonna commit suicide or go back to the air conditioning business." And somehow you come away from it with a will, with excitement, a taste.

I left the University of Iowa having started a book about Negro League baseball players called *The Bingo Long Traveling All-Stars and Motor Kings*. I thought it was a good idea and had about four or five chapters completed and I liked it. But I also had to get on with my life, get a job, make some money. And somehow still be a writer. I went to Chicago and tried to get work as a newspaper reporter. I figured I could do that and work on my novel on weeknights and weekends. I desperately wanted to be a member of the *Chicago Daily News*, the *Chicago Tribune*, or the *Chicago Sun-Times*, to become a part of the newspaper fraternity in Chicago, alongside writers such as Ben Hecht and *The Front Page* crew, Mike Royko, and the rest. I would have given anything to be a part of it.

I was finally hired by a small newspaper chain called Lerner Newspapers. They made me a general and police reporter, and they sent me out to do anything and write as many stories as I could come up with at $4.65 an hour. So I went to police station houses, to Mafia funerals, to the courts, the jails, and I developed a writer's eye because I saw so much stuff that was raw and tough and wild. Big city.

I became what I refer to as a professional coward. I loved watching other people commit mayhem. I said, "Go ahead with that manslaughter, I'll just take notes." The test of a writer, of course, is if he sees a fellow walking down the street who drops into a manhole. If he goes off and dials 911, he's a good person. If he goes over and takes notes, he's a writer. I was a writer.

About that time, Mike Royko, who is the lead columnist at the *Tribune* today and at that time was with the *Daily News*, was looking for a leg man. A leg man is the guy who does all the dirty work, goes everywhere, talks to everybody, gives the stuff to Royko and Royko turns it into a column and gets all the credit for it. But still, if you get the job as a leg man, you're in. You're part of the fraternity, and I desperately wanted that job.

I'll never forget interviewing with Royko. I brought all my stuff from

Michigan and Iowa. I put it in front of him and he read it. He said, "I'll get back with you quick, kid." He did the very next day. His secretary said, "Close, but no cigar. You didn't get the job."

So I went on with my newspaper job and continued to write *Bingo Long*. It was published, bought by the movies, and all that good stuff, and I decided to jump off and become a professional writer, a free-lancer. I got a contract to do another book and magazine articles, and a few years later, I was asked by *Esquire* magazine to do a profile of Mike Royko. I said, "Vengeance is mine, saith the kid."

I called Royko and he said, "*Esquire*. That's terrific. Let's get together." This was about four years after the job interview, my novel had come out, and I was well into another one. I sat down in his office and I said, "Mike, I have one personal question. Why didn't you hire me?" He said, "I'll tell you. I remember it very well. There are two reasons. One: I read your stuff, which was terrific, and I never hire anybody who can write better than me. Two: I knew you were working on the book on the Negro Leagues and I knew it would be a big success. I knew you'd become a novelist and have a career as a writer, but not if I hired you and you became stuck in the newspaper business. Put it this way, kid: I *made* you."

In the years that followed, I've been a professional writer and free-lance writer, and have done just about anything I wanted to. It is a wonderful job because you've got no boss and it's awful because you've got no boss. It's a great life of total freedom and it's horrible because you've got too much freedom. People ask me what it's like to be a free-lance writer and I answer with a quote from Billy Wilder, the famous producer. "They ask me what it's like to be a producer in Hollywood and I tell them it's getting up at ten o'clock in the morning and going out to the pool with a Bloody Mary and a couple of long-legged blondes until it's time to take lunch with another producer. I return from lunch and go back to the pool, have a few drinks with the same blondes, and call it a day. It's true. Eat your hearts out."

Well, not really. I lied. My favorite quote about the free-lance writing life comes from John McPhee, the fine writer and essayist, who said, "I come into the office at 8:30 in the morning and I leave at 8:30 at night. During this time I'm allegedly writing. If I'm lucky, I do two or three hours of work a day. In the meantime, I slowly go nuts." McPhee also said to help him work he ties himself to his chair with the belt of his bath-robe.

Now that, to me, is more like it. You do get out. You do meet people. I've done articles on everybody from Oprah Winfrey to Paul Harvey to Phil Donahue to Mary Tyler Moore. My existence, I think, is an attempt to be a total writer, to look at everything, at the world in its totality. You are a sponge. You soak up everything. You're interested in everything. You're an expert in something for a day or for a month or for a year. You have a passion. You have a passion for whatever it is you're writing about. You love it. You're obsessed with it. You can't get your mind off it. The total writer can't get enough of words. You can't read enough. Have you ever had the situation where you picked up a book and you loved it so much that you were totally jealous of the writer? I hate this writer. This is so good. I've had that experience often, with Eudora Welty and Flannery O'Connor and Elmore Leonard and on and on.

The total writer delights in words, phrases, and bad puns. Have you ever heard of the Bulwer-Lytton Contest? It's one of my favorites, named after the Victorian novelist Edward Bulwer-Lytton who started a novel with that famous line "It was a dark and stormy night." Well, they have a competition each year for the best "worst" first lines. This year's finalists came out recently and every writer had to have laughed out loud when he read the winner. It was in the romance novel category. I quote: "As the newest Lady Turnpot descended into the kitchen wrapped only in her celery-green dressing gown, her creamy bosom rising and falling like a temperamental soufflé, her tart mouth pursed in distaste, the sous-chef whispered to the scullery boy, 'I don't know what to make of her.'"

You have to love that as a writer. You have to delight in that. The second-place winner was almost as good. It was in the detective novel category and it went like this: "The dirty gray sky hung over the city like the sneeze shield on God's salad bar. . . . "

It's a life of words; it's a life of puns. You put your fist in the air when you come up with one like that.

Now, after doing this for about twenty years, I admit, painful as it is, I'm no longer a kid. I'm a writer, yes, in middle age. It's a little daunting. I'm not as reckless as I was. I'm not as cocksure. I'm a little gray. I'm a little slow.

I remember writing my second novel, *City Dogs*, when I was twenty-seven years old. I was thinking, considering, trying to figure out how old I should make my main character, and I thought, maybe I should make him forty-five. Forty-five, that puffy, tired, jaded, over-the-hill, withered age. I thought to myself, "No, that's too old. What could he do?" I really couldn't imagine anybody that old being a character who could do much.

Middle age sets in with a writer, as I guess it sets in with most artists, and it tempers things. It really does. It may be the reason that we get together at conferences, to share things, to recharge, to figure out what we're going to do as writers and individuals. What do you expect from yourself? Are you just marking time in your job and waiting to get out? Are you phoning in your part, counting the days until retirement? Or, if you are in retirement, are you not excited about anything?

If you're a writer, however, you have an advantage, because you can transcend the malaise. You are ageless as a writer, if you want to be. Totally ageless. Dr. Seuss never grew up. He never did. God bless him and his green eggs and ham.

As a writer you can transcend age, you can transcend infirmity, because each new book, each new article, each new project is a new start. It's a new baby. It mewls and pukes and does all those good things that come with a fresh start. That's the advantage we as writers have over other folks. I have written books about the Mafia and Sam Giancana; about anthropology and Peking Man; about Johnny Bench, the former baseball star; about trading in the commodity pits – and each one was exciting and new. A baby that was born, nurtured, and brought into maturity.

It is very exciting, challenging, fickle. On the other hand, do you get the sense that as writers we may be dinosaurs? We may be wheezing a little bit? I don't have to tell you what's been happening in this country in this last twenty years, with video stores cropping up like stinkweeds on every corner. You get the impression that if you still like to read you are a fossil, that you're rowing against the current, that you're playing the harpsichord when there are new pianos all over the place.

It can be depressing, because the novel is not as powerful as it was years ago when a book appeared and everybody was reading it, struck by it. It seldom happens anymore, because of television, because of the movies and the video age. We have to deal with that, particularly with our kids. Words are not as compelling or as quick or as immediate as television and videos.

Today I don't think every kid wants to be a writer. I don't think any kid wants to be a writer. The profession is more like classical music: it's admired and listened to, but not generally sought after. Not many kids today say, "I want to be the next Vladimir Horowitz." We just don't hear that.

A recent bookseller's survey found that 60 percent of all Americans do not visit a bookstore in a given year. This is a depressing figure. It cuts into you and makes you wonder if what you're doing as a writer is still viable.

My antidote for that – antidote as opposed to anecdote – is to go to your passions. If writing means something to you it is probably because reading means something to you. I'm convinced reading will always be that way. It is capable of stirring emotions, kindling fires within us – with a hero, a scene, a moment that somehow changes us or makes a difference. So you take your writing and you heighten it, you celebrate it, you heighten and celebrate your life.

I've taken my passions and turned them into my writing. I love baseball. I love mysteries. Now I'm writing mysteries set in baseball parks. A writer is a god, as you well know. You mold, you fashion, you appropriate, you take little events and you bring life into them, you enhance them. You take the power of memory, you fabricate, you turn it into something that means something not only to you but to other people, your readers. Let me explain.

In 1974 my wife and I went to Spain. We went to the town of Granada. In Granada is the Alhambra, the Moorish fortification. As we were touring, we came across this young boy. It was up in the hills and this kid, this little huckster, came up to us and called us "honeymooners." With a great accent he said to us, "You have seen Granada. You have seen Alhambra. Now you must come with me and see the caves. Flamenco. You must see the dancing, drink the wine. You must hear the guitars, honeymooners. You have not seen Granada until you see this." Of course, it was all for a price, some outrageous sum.

But we did it. We followed him up into the hill. We went into the cave and we watched as his sisters, who were quite overweight, danced horrible flamenco in outfits that had safety pins keeping them together despite the various bulges on their bodies. We drank very bad red wine in dirty glasses and we listened to an old man play the guitar underneath the Spanish sky. He didn't play too well. As I said, we paid an exorbitant sum for all this and we came back to the hotel and laughed heartily.

Eighteen years later, I was writing a book called *Bleeding Dodger Blue*, in which my main character was Duffy House. He's a retired sportswriter and he's full of memories. He's also a widower. He's lost his wife and he is alone, and he talks about this in his writing. He is in Los Angeles where there have been several murders, and he's trying to find out why. In the course of trying to solve these murders, he stays at the house of his friend, Joe Start. Joe is divorced and also living alone. It is a free place to stay. Start lives in the town of Alhambra, a suburb of Los Angeles. I wrote this in *Bleeding Dodger Blue:*

Joe Start's house smelled like the inside of an old book. Windows stuck shut, cobwebs stretched taut across lampshades, a refrigerator full of expired dates. Start lived at the *Times* and ate in restaurants; his house caught him every night like a backstop. It was a handsome place – full of unpainted woodwork, high ceilings, and a wide oak staircase leading upstairs from the center of the first floor – but it was stiff with neglect. As I walked around, the floors creaked as if they were happy just to have the exercise.

I went upstairs to check in. Joe's bedroom door was open, and from the hallway I could see that the insides were not pretty. My quarters were two doors down, a spare bedroom with a single bed and a single window. On one wall was a color poster of Jerry West, and on another wall was a color poster of Don Sutton. Both had been autographed to "Eddie." The room was obviously the former domain of Joe's kid, and Eddie Start liked his heroes blond.

The bed was mush, but the sheets were clean, even if they did smell of cardboard. A pair of lonely track trophies had so much dust on them that the figures looked my age. Any minute now I expected a bat to fly out of the shadows. From the window I could see tree leaves and buds and lots of other chlorophyll holders. With a grunt that shot a lance through my aching neck, I opened the window and got a breeze. The whole house needed a breeze. But that was okay. To a freeloader like me, the place was the Ritz. I unpacked my travel wardrobe and settled in.

While there was not a living plant or a piece of interior decorating newer than the Dodgers '77 yearbook, the house was crammed with books, magazines, and televisions. Whole walls in the living room and den were lined with volumes – sports, history, current affairs, literature. Stacks of magazines on everything from foreign affairs to pro football littered the floor like boulders. And I counted a television in every downstairs room – a red one sat atop the refrigerator – except the toilet. There were magazines there.

I nosed around a little and nursed my neck with a hot towel. I found a beaker of grapefruit juice and nursed it with vodka. In no time I was lost in peace and quiet, the house having plenty of that to spare. Grand Avenue was not Sunset Boulevard, thank goodness. I started picking through Start's library, pausing with Shelby Foote and Garry Wills, Studs Terkel, and Harry Mark Petrakis. I lingered long in something called *Toscanini's Fumble,* by a smart doctor of neurology named Harold Klawans, that told me why J. Rodney Richard, the enormous smoke-throwing pitcher for the Astros, suffered a stroke.

From a bag of rock-hard bagels in the freezer and a passable crock of cheddar cheese, I made myself dinner. I went out and sat on the front stoop and munched it to the crickets and birds and other night sounds of the neighborhood – a beautiful April evening in Alhambra. I rolled the name over my tongue. I had been to the real McCoy many years ago, stayed in a Granada hotel with a balcony view of the old Moorish palace, and walked into the hills. My lover and I succumbed to the blandishments of a gypsy boy, who for an exorbitant sum led us to a hillside cave home bedecked with copper pots, where we drank Spanish wine and listened to an old man play the classical guitar. The boy said the old man was Segovia. I sighed and put my arm around my young wife. The boy called us honeymooners. Looking around Joe Start's real estate, I could hear his Castilian lisp as clear as yesterday. There was not a soul walking on the street. Nobody to see me, an old fool, put my arm around an imaginary mate. . . .

So here's what you do: take your memories and present them to the reader. Take your passions. You take as much guilt and as little total depravity as you can safely mix in. You read. You steal. You want desperately to be a writer. You volunteer to nail your soft parts to a tree. You soak up everything. You take notes. You retire to your garret or your study or your office and you tie yourself to your chair with the belt of your bathrobe. And you write. You slowly go crazy, but you write. You drink lye, if that is what it will take, and you remember the nights and caves in Granada. Because you desperately want to be a writer. You do. You write. You write. And you write.

MIROSLAV HOLUB

The Impact of Science on "Poet's Soul"

[ASPEN WRITERS' CONFERENCE]

It is the contention of Bryan Appleyard, in *Understanding the Present* (1992), that science affronts human dignity. "Science is not a neutral or innocent commodity. . . . Rather, it is spiritually corrosive, burning away ancient authorities and traditions."

Appleyard believes that science is – or has become, since Galileo – an autonomous entity, with a life of its own, progressively detrimental to human existence. Regardless of the possible role science and technology have played in the recent triumph of liberal democracy, Appleyard and others believe science endangers human life on the planet. Liberal democracy – which makes science possible – is not a human triumph, since it allows too many things adverse to what they call "human essence": embryo research, abortion, animal experimentation, environmental destruction, atomic fission-fusion technologies, and so on.

One should state, then, what would be a human triumph, or what would have been.

In fact, this part of the argument is *de norma* and *de jure* missing in all kinds of antiscience and alternative-science points of view, orthodoxies, and movements.

More surprisingly, in all such argumentation, we miss the definition of "human essence" as well. If it is something unchanging at the core of each man, woman, and child, what is wrong with, say, animal experimentation, since so many ancient – and present – ethnic groups indulged in animal and human sacrifice, compared to which a surgical intervention in an anesthetized animal is a pastoral procedure?

If, on the other hand, this "human essence" is a changing quality in each of us, which I firmly believe – so that "human," "being human," "humanism," and "humanitarian" are expressions with a changing content – how can we regret, as Appleyard does, that ancient authorities and traditions have been burned away? How can we suggest that any kind of fundamentalism – religious, ecological, or ethnic – is a natural trait of present "mankind" and not a relapse into more primitive human attitudes?

It was Picasso who said, "We always stick with the old-fashioned ideas, with outdated definitions, as if it were not the very task of an artist to find new ones." And he was well aware of what he was burning away.

Ultimately, then, how can we suggest that science is an autonomous, aggressive, oppressive force? On the contrary, I believe it may be as integral a component of modern humanity as art.

What was wrong with the atmosphere in Vienna during the first decades of this century, where new disciplines in the domains of the subconscious, sexuality, and language emerged, as well as new approaches to the demarcation of sciences and pseudosciences? Why should Freud and other kinds of poets be less corrosive to traditional human values than Karl Popper and Ernst Mach? Doesn't the atmosphere in Vienna – or at other times Copenhagen, Cambridge, or even Prague – show that science is not an autonomous entity, but a natural way of general human progress toward solving the soluble?

Either we respect even what we do not understand, it seems to me, or we pretend to understand only what we respect. As artists, we respect art. We may even understand art. But why, as artists, should we be menaced by science because we simply can't understand it? Sometimes we do not even try to understand.

I admit that these are the feelings or opinions of somebody who has tried, all his life, to do both things. I have been working in immunology as well as writing poetry and essays since 1954. And I know at least a few other artists, musicians, and writers who respect science as a way of acquiring knowledge and as an integral part of western culture.

What corrosive forces or, conversely, what supporting factors, then, have I experienced as a poet from the practice of science?

The main limitation I know of is that I am unable to accept any other mode of acquiring knowledge about the world of Nonself than science.

In other words, I am unable to share the myths that are listed by Milton Rothman in his book, *The Science Gap,* published in 1992:

> Nothing is known for sure.
> Nothing is impossible.
> Whatever we think we know now is likely to be overturned in the future.
> Advanced civilizations will possess forces unknown to us today.
> All theories are equal.

Neither can I accept the traditional poetic myth, "The scientist doubts, the poet knows," because, on a personal level, and in my personal experience in the laboratory, not many things are known for sure. In most situations, one is impersonating the courtier from the poem "Seekers After Truth," by Dannie Abse:

> Below, distant, the roaring courtiers
> rise to their feet – less shocked than irate.
> Salome has dropped the seventh veil
> and they've discovered there are eight.

In other words, I am not left with my private history, mentality, ingenuity, stupidity, and indolence, but share the notions established by observation, experiment, and computation – that the planet Earth is in the solar system; that there are laws of gravity; that photons are unchanging permanent entities; that one cannot exceed the speed of light; that life is based exclusively on biochemical principles, such as the self-perpetuating nucleic acids, and human existence follows the principle of Order-out-of-Chaos; and that there are only two transcendental categories in life: the genome, and the extracorporeal heredity sometimes called culture and sometimes called civilization.

All else is everyday routine, at which the man on the street is better than the intellectual, and an interplay of instincts, including the basic ones, at which we were a lot better some 200,000 years ago.

One of the possible effects of the impact of science on my soul is that I do not long to be 200,000 years older!

However, there exists some everyday, inner routine that needs the old miracles, that needs myths and howling and fairy tales, if only for dealing with these basic instincts. For me also, miracles, illogical feelings, and instincts are part of the deep or dark Self. Hence, the need for my soft-centered, poetic approach.

I don't think that these personal inner myths are great fun, as the popular metamyth goes. I don't even know whether they are good for something. Definitely, they are strictly personal and have nothing to do with eventual, collective paranoias. They are just some sort of idiosyncratic metaphors, some sort of black symbiotic plants in the "secret gardens of the self," in William Carlos Williams' terms.

Therefore, I do not doubt the role of poetry (in the broadest sense) in my life, in every life, in the inner, inaccessible world governed by principles of uncertainty. I do need poetry as a sort of consolation, temporary relief and limited hope about the immediate and distant future. I do *not* need poetry or religion, or New Age anthropology, to explain the past or present of the Self or Nonself. I do need poetry as the last possibility to say something against the inevitable, against the speed of light or the fact of gravitation, although I know that this is nonsense. That is, I need nonsense in a very deep and existential and futile way.

However, I hate nonsense as ideology – artistic ideology or any other fundamentalist ideology.

But – and this is another "limitation" of science or scientific practice – I am well aware that the real absurdity, the real surreality and the real counterpoint to the rational can be appreciated only when we have an educated, or adult, notion of the obvious, of the real, and of the point. That is to say, all that can be derived only from the basic rudiments of science in the modern mentality, not from inborn common sense as a manifestation of our perennial "humanity."

The third limitation (or impact) of science on the poet's soul is a technical one: I don't have much time to spend on the actual labor of writing. Basically, I must wait until the poem, the image, the idea is almost complete through a hardly conscious process of recalling, associations, and ideation. Science prevents one from writing much, or talking much, or struggling too long with the creative process. Rather, writing appears as some sort of recreation. This may be a pity for some poets. For me, it was good luck.

Inevitably, one must concentrate on one problem, one mode, and one kind of activity at a time to be effective or do anything like research in any sense, even the poetic one. There can be no free flotation, no vague freedom in any type of effective work. Scientific practice has taught me that there is a difference between really working and pretending to work, that ten minutes are ten minutes, even at a poetry reading, and the long social exchange of monologues can't replace actual achievement. And, finally, that criticism of the work is to be respected, always, not neglected as mischief, misunderstanding, or the plot of a convocation of dullards.

And there is a moral component derived from science. Science nowadays requires a rigorous way of thinking and a scrupulous code of behavior, as Jacob Bronowski reiterated in his essays. One is forced to meticulous, exacting activity in all scientific practice – from a biological experiment to abdominal surgery, from getting the right information and data to making the proper solution, taking exact measurements, and applying the right transistor. Above all, science obliges us to ask the right or legitimate questions, which are more essential for some kinds of survival than the eventual answers.

I do not mean that one does not acquire an exacting attitude in pursuit of the arts and humanities. But in science and technology, you simply develop an exacting attitude quicker and you are aware that deviations will be punished. I know of many cases of fraud, error, and human failure in science and technology – from somebody copying other people's work and papers, and publishing them under his or her own name, to Chernobyl. By contrast, I do not recall many frauds and failures in the arts. I suggest that it's because nobody notices them.

There are strict rules for conducting an experiment, and strict instructions about using an electronic device, just as there are limiting rules about writing a poem. The difference in our present world – however sad that difference may be – is that everybody living in a more or less civilized country acquires and observes technological rules, while not many people would even theoretically accept the essential laws of a poem. Poetry is taken as a sort of unruly behavior. The sad result is that we learn the norms of life from technical operating instructions rather than the core of our souls as manifested in poetry.

Still, I submit, it is better to have some norms and rules than to have none.

The impact of science on poet's soul is also in the practical acceptance of this sad state of affairs. At the same time, one lives, deep inside, with false and childish hopes and by false and childish hopes.

At the end of one of my poems, at the end of one of my poetry books, I conclude:

> We didn't find anything.
> But at least we may say it . . .
> Although –

This may be the general result of the impact of science on the poet's soul: listless realism, together with that ever-limiting "Although."

JAMES D. HOUSTON

A Writer's Sense of Place

[THE SQUAW VALLEY COMMUNITY OF WRITERS WORKSHOPS]

In writing workshops, a large part of the conversation focuses on personal relationships and matters of kinship—the husband and the wife, the mother and the daughter, the father and the son, or the absent father, or the missing lover, or the seducer, the seducee. There are good and necessary reasons for this, since this is the basic stuff of fiction: what we do to each other, and with each other.

For a few minutes today I want to talk about another kind of kinship. Each time I drive up into these mountains, climb from sea-level to six thousand feet and see the bowl of peaks rising all around us, I get reawakened to the power and the magic of landscape and open country and to the many ways that certain places can work on us. When Oakley Hall asked, "If you had to give a talk at the conference this year, what would it be?", I said that by Sunday afternoon I would probably be ready to free-associate about The Sense of Place.

By *place* I don't mean simply names and points of interest as identified on a map. What has fascinated me for a long time now is the relationship between a locale and the lives lived there, the relationship between terrain and the feelings it can call out of us, the way a certain place can provide us with grounding, location, meaning, can bear upon the dreams we dream, can sometimes shape our view of history.

The idea of place is nothing new, of course. It has been a constant in human life from day one. You can't avoid it. You have to park somewhere and get a roof over your head, and wherever this happens has to be a place of one kind or another. But we're not always aware of it as such. At some point, place moves into the conscious life. When that occurs we begin to have a sense of it, an awareness of it and our relationship to it.

I have lived most of my life on the West Coast, between San Francisco, where I was born, and Monterey Bay, where we've been based for the past thirty years. It is clearly my home region, a stretch of coastline and coastal mountain ranges I now think of as my natural habitat. But I did not always see it this way. For many years I did not see it at all. I had to leave home and travel around the country, see a lot of other places, go out to the Hawaiian Islands, go to Mexico and to Europe. Looking back, I think I can now isolate my own moment of awakening, when I finally began to see and to contemplate my habitat.

This was in the mid-1960s, a couple of years after we moved to Santa Cruz and I was trying to get started as a writer – which involved a lot of pacing and staring out the window.

In an interview once, someone asked Bruce Jay Friedman why he had chosen this particular career, and he said, "Because it allows me to use the word *work* to describe my greatest pleasure in life."

"You mean writing," the interviewer said.

"I mean brooding," Friedman said, "and pacing back and forth and staring out the window."

Early in 1964, soon after I had finished graduate work at Stanford and we had moved from the Peninsula over the hill to the coast, I was brooding and pacing back and forth, trying to finish a short story about Sweden that I had started during my Air Force time in England, five years earlier. As I paused to stare out the window, I noticed a candy store that stood on a corner about a block away, on the far side of a large open lot, empty except for a few neglected fruit trees. We had been living in that house for a couple of years, and I had been visiting the town of Santa Cruz off and on since high school, so I had seen this candy store a hundred times, maybe a thousand times. Yet I had not seen it. I had never looked at it, a fixture in my daily life so familiar it had gone entirely unnoticed.

As I studied the details – the whitewashed walls, the corny Dutch windmill with its tiny window flashing in the sun – something began to buzz, the tingling across my scalp that I refer to as the literary buzz, a little signal from the top of my head that there is some mystery here, or some unrevealed linkage that will have to be explored with words.

I sat down at my typing machine and began to describe the candy store. By the time I finished, fifteen pages later, I had described the stream of cars along the shoreline road that runs through the neighborhood, I had described the town, and where I thought it fit into some larger patterns of northern California and the West. I had begun to examine, as well, why I had chosen this town and this stretch of coast, and the elderly, windblown house we still occupy.

The result was an essay both regional and personal. In terms of my perception of myself as a writer and what I could write about, it was a small but crucial turning point. It was my first attempt to write not only *about* this part of the world, but to write *from* this part of the world. This also turned out to be the first piece I sold to a national magazine, which seemed at the time to validate the impulses that had propelled the writing. It came out in the now-defunct *Holiday*, making it the first piece to earn anything like a significant amount of money, six hundred dollars – a decent fee for an essay back in the mid-1960s, and a bonanza for us, in the days when four hundred was our monthly budget.

Since then the sense of region and place has played an ever larger role in what I've chosen to write about, both in nonfiction and in fiction. As far as storytelling goes, in the most general terms, I think there are two ways it can work. Sometimes a character in the story has a conscious sense of place. More often it is the writer who has the sense of place, or who grasps the relationship between a life and a locale. In *The Grapes of Wrath*, to take a famous example, John Steinbeck knows the layout of the San Joaquin Valley. He knows the water systems, the fertility of the soil, the appeal of the soil, and the role of agriculture in the region's history. He also knows the power of the legend that has drawn the Joad family west from Oklahoma. He knows a lot more about this than the Joads themselves know or have time to think about, since they have so recently arrived and their full attention is on survival. A large part of the novel's concern might be described as a dialogue between their struggle and the magnetic power of the place they've been drawn to – the natural endowments of that place, the dream that has attached to it, and the irony or the underside of that dream.

In recent years I've been working on a sequence of novels tied to the terrain of northern California, in which the lives of one family have been much affected by this terrain. In these novels there is always a character whose personal sense of place is central to the story. The first of these was *Continental Drift*, published by Knopf in 1978. It's set in the coast range near Monterey Bay. It's a family saga, a love story, a murder story, an exploration of the geography and the geology. The title, of course, refers to the global pattern of tectonic plates and fracture lines that has helped us to understand the profound feature of the continent's western edge we call the San Andreas fault. It also provides the novel's metaphor. Via the fault line, the landscape of California has its built-in disaster factor; and yet this same landscape, due to the same forces that created the fault line, continues to be a source of nourishment and even spiritual sustenance. Call it the yin and yang of coastal geology.

The central character is a fellow named Montrose Doyle. He is forty-six. With his wife and two sons he presides over fifty-five acres of orchard and grazing land that borders the San Andreas, which has given him a way of thinking about where he lives and – in this passage from the novel's early pages – thinking about The Big One:

Is Montrose a fatalist? Yes. And no. He anticipates. Yet he does not anticipate. What he loves to dwell on is that steady creep which, a few million years hence, will put his ranch on a latitude with Juneau, Alaska. He admires the foresight of the Spanish cartographers who, in their earliest maps, pictured California as an island. Sometimes late at night, after he has been drinking heavily, he will hike out to his fence line and imagine that he can feel beneath his feet the dragging of the continental plates, and imagine that he is standing on his own private raft, a New World Noah, heading north, at two inches per year.

Most of the time he doesn't think about it at all. It is simply there, a presence beneath his land. If it ever comes to mind during his waking hours he thinks of it as just that, a presence, a force, you might even say a certainty, one thing he knows he can count on – this relentless grinding of two great slabs which have been butting head-on now for millennia and are now about to relax.

There is a companion novel to *Continental Drift*. It's called *Love Life* and it came out in 1985, also from Knopf. It's not a sequel. But maybe it qualifies as a spin-off, since it deals with the same territory, the Santa Cruz Mountains, and members of the same family, in this case the older son of Montrose Doyle, and this son's wife, Holly. They are both thirty-two, married ten years, with two kids. *Love Life* is the wife's story, Holly's story, told in her voice, and it begins on the day she discovers that her husband, Grover, is involved with a younger woman. So this too is a family drama, but with quite a bit of geography mixed in.

The crisis in their relationship is linked to a crisis in the environment. The story is set during a devastating winter storm that comes in off the Pacific and leaves them isolated at the end of their river valley road. The bridges are out, hillsides crumble, phone lines and power lines are down. At a time when they both want nothing more than to get away from each other, they are in fact trapped by the mud and the water and tree trunks that come crashing across their road.

Part of what gets Holly through it is her sense of place. As narrator and as a central character, she is attuned to the features of her region, her habitat—the light, the creek, the trees, the nearest hills. I wanted to get this established right at the outset. In the opening pages, before we meet her husband or her kids, we are looking out her early morning window:

An orange light had set our bedroom curtains smoldering. The curtains were orange. When it wasn't raining they smoldered most of the time, which is what I had hoped for when I bought them at Macy's. But this light passing through the window seemed about to burst them into flame. I drew them back and saw the sun filling a low notch in the eastern hills, the sun's most southerly point, only rising through that notch for a couple of weeks before starting north again. If I had been asleep for twenty years and had awakened that morning, I would have known the season in an instant, the month, perhaps the week, by the sun's angle and the winter clarity of its flame, igniting curtains, backlighting the camelia bushes and the spindly saplings I had planted on the slope behind the house, backlighting the creek whose waters then were high enough and full enough to make a glossy surface under the trees, and backlighting the light itself, so that all the air around the house and above the creek and all the air between the window and the farthest ridge seemed polished by this ball of new fire.

I'd like to move away from works of fiction now and make a few, more general comments. The idea that a place can have holding power or be some kind of sustaining factor in a person's life is not widely agreed upon. In fact, it is an idea most Americans nowadays are out of touch with. There are a lot of reasons for this: the concept of private property, for example. It's a useful concept, up to a point. But if you're not careful, it leads to the idea of real estate, which in turn tends to promote the view of land or property as a commodity, as something to be bought and sold, rather than a place to be inhabited and respected. In this country we are also extremely mobile. It's not unusual to move five, six, seven times. We are a restless nation, and from this mobility and restlessness has come a whole fiction of *dis*placement, which accounts for a great deal of what is being written these days – a vast literary subject unto itself.

Meanwhile, there are still places you can visit in the United States that have been inhabited for centuries by people who have more or less stayed put. At Taos Pueblo, north of Santa Fe, people have been a continuous presence for more than eight hundred years. On the north shore of the Big Island of Hawaii there is a temple site called Mo'okini, laid out fifteen hundred years ago. According to their genealogy chart, one Hawaiian family has provided the guardians for this site, in unbroken lineage, since 500 A.D.

Luckily for the rest of us, histories like these have kept alive the idea that a place can have power, sustaining power, shaping power, sometimes sacred power. When voices in touch with these places and their traditions speak to us, more and more of us tend to listen, because there is a yearning now to reconnect with the power that resides in the places of earth, to remember things we have forgotten. No matter where you live these days, some feature of the nearby landscape is under siege – the river, the forest, the seashore, something. This in itself forces us to become better informed, pay closer attention, look at what's right around us before it's changed too drastically or perhaps gone forever. The knowledge that we can lose our places has quickened our sense of place. The knowledge that the entire planet is now endangered has quickened our sense of the precariousness of the Earth and the need to honor and respect all its systems and its habits.

A while back I was talking with my friend, Frank La Pena, who heads the Native American Studies program at Sacramento State University. He grew up farther north, in a region bounded by the McCloud River, Redding, and Mount Shasta, traditionally the home territory of his people, the Wintu. They have called that region home for more than ten thousand years.

Frank is a man so deeply rooted you can almost think the Western

earth speaks through him. He likes to talk about Shasta, which dominates the landscape in Wintu country. For him this fourteen-thousand-
foot volcanic peak is much more than a dramatic landmark and photographer's delight, much more than a challenge for climbers and skiers. It is
a holy place he approaches with reverence. For him the mountain can be
a kind of mentor. It can also serve as chapel and sanctuary. He told me
about a pilgrimage he made to the mountain when a favorite uncle passed
away. Frank went on foot and left behind a lock of his own hair as he expressed his grief and prayed for safe passage. For the Wintu, who call
themselves "the mountain/river people," Shasta is the final point of contact with this world, and the gateway to the next.

When I heard that story I envied Frank, and I told him so. I told him
that after the Loma Prieta quake in October of 1989 – with its epicenter
just eight miles from our home – I had been filled with fear and runaway
anxiety and, for a while, a sense of betrayal. I longed then for a place I
could go and stand and voice my fear and release my anxiety and make
some kind of peace with the powers residing in the earth.

"As you tell me about your pilgrimage to the mountain," I said, "I realize what a yearning I have in my life for that kind of ritual or for that
kind of relationship. I wish my culture provided me with more guidance
in this area, but it doesn't."

I was astounded by his reply. "You don't have to deprive yourself of
that," he said. "It is really up to you. It is always available. You can
awaken that aspect of a place, if you make your own connection with it."

It is really up to you. This was a truly liberating idea – that I could
awaken the sacred aspect of a place, or at least open the way to this possibility. What it means is being awakened to that place in myself, that possibility in myself, and allowing the openness to such a dialogue.

The key word here, I think, is dialogue. And maybe this is what can
bring my rambling digression back to fiction-making and storytelling.
Very often *place* functions primarily as setting, as background for the action. That is its role, and that's okay; the emphasis in the piece is located
somewhere else. But from time to time you come across a story where the
place is profoundly felt, as a feature of the narrative that is working on the
characters or through the characters or is somehow bearing upon their
lives. I think of works by Wallace Stegner, Willa Cather, Eudora Welty,
Edward Abbey, James Welch, William Kittredge, Leslie Marmon Silko,

Rudolfo Anaya. Our literature is rich with such works, stories wherein at least part of what's going on is some form of dialogue between a place – whether it be an island or a mountain or a city or a shoreline or a subregion of the continent – and the lives being lived. I look upon this as one more version of the endless dialogue we're all involved in, between the human imagination and the world we find ourselves inhabiting and continually trying to understand.

SIDNEY BURRIS

Auden's Generalizations

[SEWANEE WRITERS' CONFERENCE]

Occasionally we encounter a writer who has a gift for memorable speech, and even those of us with the most mundane memories find ourselves accurately recalling those lines whose mangled versions we had long ago confronted in the colloquial idiom. We seem always to have known, for example, that death's relationship to beauty is vaguely maternal, or that good friends, if they want to retain their cordiality, had best keep good fences, or that learning, when administered in little doses, is a dangerous potion. "So that's where that phrase comes from!" we have often said to ourselves when we encounter it in its original context, as if the writer in question had stolen it from the conversations we had been carrying on for years. And in one sense we are right. Generalizations of this sort become the common property of all those who would use them. As they insinuate themselves into our conversation, finding an inalienable home in our working vocabularies, they exercise the ungracious liberty of denying their authors. Such phrases have outlasted their individual, laboring creators, and once they have achieved this level of currency, they provide evidence for one of the paradoxes that attend the literary arts: literary creation depends upon the extreme indulgence of the individual personality, but these memorable phrases, the happy results of such an indulgence, often achieve anonymity, a kind of literary vagrancy. That a little learning is a dangerous thing seems less an individual author's opinion than a canonical command, and as we submit to the odd persuasions of a phrase, we abandon the territorial economies of the individual personality, and mimic for a moment the action of transcendence.

Relegated to its inferior station by the towering authority of the single line, the original context often suffers from such transcendence. Let a bell begin to peal, have someone describe it as tolling, and most will think of Hemingway, a few will think of Donne, and some fewer still will feel unwittingly lugubrious, but all will perceive the nimbus that marks the phrase "for whom the bells tolls" for special consideration. In any case, the original text from which it is drawn, one of Donne's "Meditations," has long ago been sloughed off, and we are left with this authoritarian phrase, freewheeling through our hoard of memorable quotations and enjoying a life irreversibly severed from the specific subjects that had originally engaged its author.

Aside from the occasional scholar or pedant, no one laments the measure of autonomy that has been granted to these lines and phrases. Even the most trivial pleasure gleaned from intoning these magical formulas is a pleasure that we abandon at our peril. But now and again, one of them warrants an explication because the phrase in question has been so crudely mined from its original setting that its current reception is simply wrongheaded. The poem that I have in mind is W. H. Auden's "In Memory of W. B. Yeats," and the line, "For poetry makes nothing happen. . . ." The typical response to this line was recently given its full-spirited incarnation as the opening paragraph of an essay in one of our leading literary quarterlies. The writer, Samuel Hazo, is concerned to point out that contemporary American poetry is in a sorry way because many fine poets are underrated and many bad poets are overrated. This imbalance has been partly conceived and executed, of course, by Harold Bloom and – what harangue now is credible without her? – Helen Vendler, but to these well-known enemies of American verse he also adds a shadowy group labeled their "Manhattan counterparts." The culprits, then, are two scholars and a borough of New York City. But standing behind this allegiance, as the Great Society stood behind the recent Los Angeles riots, is W. H. Auden and his infamous line:

"Poetry makes nothing happen." Ever since W. H. Auden wrote this vapid line in his otherwise memorable elegy for William Butler Yeats, numerous American and British poets have been writing in ways to prove him correct. Part of the fault can be traced to the influence of Auden himself on these writers. To put aside his astuteness as a critic . . . he remained a poet whose poems often seemed to be commentaries on the emotions he evoked, not expressions of the emotions themselves. . . . Poetry written in this vein is not the "true voice of feeling" that Herbert Read said it should be but frequently is the mere versification of thought. It conveys the after-the-fact wisdom of the commentator, not the experiencer, even though all poets know that they must be experiencers with the ability to re-create their experiences in words that enable others to feel what they have felt. . . .

When Auden said that poetry made nothing happen, he placed a colon at the end of the four words in question, and although his concern for punctuation – like Yeat's – was casual at best, readers can confidently expect the lines that follow to elucidate those that have just preceded. What Auden composed to follow his famous pronouncement must figure in any final assessment:

> For poetry makes nothing happen: it survives
> In the valley of its saying where executives
> Would never want to tamper; it flows south
> From ranches of isolation and the busy griefs,
> Raw towns that we believe and die in; it survives,
> A way of happening, a mouth.

So what *does* poetry do? Poetry "survives," a virtue that in 1939 was hardly a trivial matter, and it "flows"; it remains an adaptable communication whose strength lies in its ability to transcend the suffocating culture represented in this passage by the "executives" and – in a poem begun eleven months later, "New Year Letter" – by the "Empiric, Economic Man." Such charges smack of the radical decade that gave birth to Auden's career, but Marxism for Auden never quickened an authentic revolutionary sensibility; his Marxism was indelibly streaked by his allegiances to various psychological models of the time, and the resulting position caused him predictably to internalize the rusting landscapes of ruined capitalistic cities – Marxist economic theory ironically threatened Auden's inner life. The passage then ends with two phrases set in apposition to the pronoun "it," here representing the noun poetry – poetry, Auden writes, ultimately involves a "way of happening, a mouth." Auden depicts his art as a fully integrated epistemology, a cognitive process *in* which things happen, not one that *makes* things happen. Poetry, in fact, circumscribes an arena far larger than that of simple social engagement. It is "a way of happening" that avoids the grosser negotiations of cause and effect, of simple persuasion. According to Auden, poetry – or literature, for that matter – cannot reliably and consistently bring about political, economic, or social change in a predictable way. Because its effects are largely unpredictable, it is useless in securing a specific goal, in making something happen. Someone normally at this point brings up Goethe's novel *The Sorrows of Young Werther*, a book that encouraged several young Germans to end their lives precipitously and, the argument runs, if that is not a case of literature making something happen, then what is? Yes, of course, the answer must go, but that novel still does not qualify as a reliable means of killing someone, of making something dire and final happen. Planting the novel on your enemy's bedside table is a grossly inefficient way of getting rid of him, and writers must not flatter themselves that their verbal contraptions can compete in the world of powerfully physical negotiations. Poetry makes nothing happen consistently and reliably, although it can on occasion produce explicit results.

But Auden's infamous pronouncement derives from his controversial, criticized, and largely unpopular strategy of delivering such pronouncements with regularity and ease. Hazo's contention that much of Auden's verse tends toward the poetry of commentary rather than the poetry of experience belongs to the traditional line of dissent that begins roughly with Randall Jarrell's observation in 1945 that Auden "moralizes interminably." What Hazo disparagingly recognizes in Auden's verse as an "after-the-fact wisdom" represents, to my way of thinking, an extensive attempt to restore to contemporary poetry its old machinery of metaphysical argumentation. Certainly, contemporary readers must retool their ears for it, and they must disarm a few of their modernist expectations if they are to understand this aspect of his poetry. But Auden, unlike his immediate predecessors, was acutely aware of the deeply influential model of Romantic poetics inherited by the twentieth century. The kind of domineering subjectivity of Shelley's "Alastor," for example, remains uncomfortably close to the moody ruminations of Eliot's "The Love Song of J. Alfred Prufrock." In his attempt to find different wellsprings from which his own verse might issue, Auden entertained the idea of circumventing, or at least ameliorating, the influence of much early nineteenth-century poetic theory by resuscitating certain argumentative practices that are most closely associated with the eighteenth century, particularly with Dryden's measured public voice, or with Pope's argumentative wit in *An Essay on Criticism*.

Yet nowadays the suggestion becomes more and more plausible that Auden simply lacked the language to effect such a leap. He certainly knew that his inherited model of selfhood, however he might submit it to the various psychological perspectives that were current in the early decades of the century, ultimately came down to him from an entrenched Romantic self-consciousness. Auden's problem is a perennial one. In a recent issue of *The Nation*, Gore Vidal addresses the effects of monotheism on our public discourse – the language available to us to carry out rigorous analyses of our weaknesses – and he finds our problem to be essentially a linguistic one:

> It is very easy to discuss *what* has gone wrong with us. It is not so easy to discuss what should be done to correct what has gone wrong. It is absolutely impossible in our public discourse to discuss *why* so much has gone wrong and, indeed, has been wrong with us since the very beginning of the country, and even before that when our white tribes were living elsewhere.

Vidal's point here, that certain moral or ethical issues remain impervious to our explications because we have lost the discourse to carry out such a project, has been for some time one of the essential notions propounded by pragmatist thinkers, of whom none is more representative than Richard Rorty. In 1986, in *The London Review of Books*, Rorty wrote:

> The mind of Europe did not *decide* to accept the idiom of Romantic poetry, or of socialist politics, or of Galilean mechanics. That sort of shift was no more an act of will than a result of argument. Rather, Europe gradually lost the habit of using certain words and gradually acquired the habit of using others.

A good deal of Auden's poetry, particularly that which Jarrell characterized as moralizing interminably, situates itself between two very distinct linguistic habits, which I will clarify in a moment. But if, as Rorty and others argue, these habits have traditionally determined the subjects that we are able to discuss and relegated to obscurity those we are unable to discuss, then our century's fascination with psychological motivation seems plausible and necessary. Why these particular habits and not those particular habits? Auden plunged headlong, as have all of us, into the psychological sciences to excavate his answers, and once there, finding the individual, disintegrated psyche, he recognized the old Romantic obsession with subjective introspection, a poetics of contingency that had early on begun to seem inadequate to him. For Auden, the development of a theory of poetry began increasingly to embrace an ethical project that would deploy its poetry in certain characteristic ways.

Auden had gradually been preparing himself for a return to the Anglican church, and on or around October 1940 Auden openly embraced the religious beliefs and practices of his childhood. This was the time of the "swift and crashing destruction of Poland" – the phrase is Churchill's – and Auden's annunciation could not have been entirely unexpected by his friends. "The English intellectuals," he said to Erika Mann's brother, Golo, "who now cry to Heaven against the evil incarnated in Hitler have no Heaven to cry to. . . . " During 1940, Auden expressed a similar sentiment in a more political sense, writing that "the whole trend of liberal thought has been to undermine faith in the absolute . . . it has tried to make reason the judge. . . . But since life is a changing process . . . the attempt to find a humanistic basis for keeping a promise, works logically with the conclusion, 'I can break it whenever I feel it convenient.'" For the time being, Auden became an avid and serious reader of theology, but he avoided public espousals of dogma, and once remarked that arguments designed to prove or disprove the existence of God are "returned unopened to the sender." Having inherited the language – or to use Rorty's term, the habit – of psychological crisis that characterized both Romantic and modernist writing, Auden was now attempting to inherit another habit, another way of speaking, that would serve as a counter to the modernist idiom. Auden's task became not so much an attempt to identify and naturalize what he had inherited (a sizable project in itself); it became more of a full-scale attempt to assign value to his inheritance, and to do so by summoning up a language, or again, a habit, that would engulf his poetic inheritance. By the simple process of juxtaposition, then, his new language would evaluate and determine the worth of his inherited tradition. For the first time in almost two centuries, English poetry in Auden's hands attempted to formulate an accessible ethical argument.

Almost coincident with Auden's return to the church, and perhaps the best *apologia* of his return, "New Year Letter" was completed in April 1940 and dedicated to Elizabeth Mayer, a German immigrant who along with her husband had fled Nazi persecution. The poem dedicated to Mayer falls into three sections comprising more than one thousand lines of octosyllabic couplets, and most of its readers have been quick – and I think correct – to relegate it to an Augustan tradition of epistolary poetry. One characteristic of epistolary verse pertains directly to this discussion: such poetry normally involved two intended readers, one specific, one general. Auden's poem, while addressed specifically to Mayer, is available "to all / Who wish to read it anywhere." This particular structure informs most ethical discourse as well. A series of general arguments concerning human behavior are developed – available "to all / Who wish to read it" – but they are arguments that envision specific and individual application.

To be fair to Auden's poem – and to be fair to ourselves as readers of it – we must recognize immediately the most important assumption of the poem. It lies buried without much of a marker in Part Two where Auden is pondering the nature of evil, particularly in its manifestation as Mephistopheles. Auden writes:

> Against his paralysing smile
> And honest realistic style
> Our best protection is that we
> In fact live in eternity.

We in fact live in eternity! How are we to take such a statement? We can, if we like, dismiss it out of hand. But as an assertion in ethical discourse, it presents formidable challenges for a secular ethics because if we accept the assertion – which as sympathetic readers of the poem, we must, even if momentarily – the assertion legitimizes with one fell swoop two thousand years of moral philosophy set in motion by the Resurrection. Auden's statement that we live in eternity might well have satisfied St. Paul, but St. Paul would not have been satisfied with the ethical climate in which Auden made his statement, and in fact if we view our climate as comprising a set of qualifications different from those that attended St. Paul's assertion, Auden's identical assertion will have different implications. We might be tempted to say that eternal life is eternal life, but we, as did Auden, know better. To utter such a broadly applicable generalization requires, at the very least, that contemporary readers evaluate it by placing it among the constellation of competing assertions that have become the stock-in-trade of this particular sort of dialogue.

One of our ablest ethical philosophers, Jeffrey Stout, has described succinctly in another context the sort of terrain that Auden traverses in his poem. In *Ethics After Babel,* Stout addresses the gradual secularization of Western culture that spread throughout Europe after the English Renaissance:

> Secularized public moral discourse may have made it more likely that disbelief would gain a foothold it didn't previously have, given how much one could now do in the culture without presupposing the existence of a specific sort of God; but it also left ample room for religious phenomena such as millennial sects, the cult of self-improvement, and the multiplication of denominations.

Interest in understanding the ways in which human beings might properly behave never waned as the church began to lose its disquisitional authority; another player simply appeared at the table now, making very legitimate demands in a very different language. As the rising sciences began to define human cognition, theology was left to tell us all we needed to know about piety and religious affectivity. The truce that eventually developed has been an uneasy but enduring one. Stout again:

> This strategy can work, however, only if two conditions obtain. Science must turn out to have no knowledge, strictly speaking, concerning God's existence and attributes, whereas theology must somehow make sense of itself without claiming such knowledge either. In other words, the eternal covenant could be effective only as long as both parties remained silent on the issue in which both were once thought to have an interest – namely, knowledge of God.

Now we are in more of a position to understand what Rorty meant when he said that European culture had gradually lost the habit of using certain words. Part of the mediated truce stipulated that for secularization to proceed smoothly, both parties, the scientists and the theologians, must agree to bracket the word "God" and its attendant idea when any comprehensive ethical system was proposed. From start to finish, "New Year Letter" attempts to remain faithful to the bargain, although it has other transgressive intentions; God, as the transcendental Christian deity, is addressed only once, and that during the closing lines of the poem in a formulaic Latin expression.

Generalizations provided for Auden the verbal evidence of ethical concord, and such concord, of course, extended into religious contexts. He once replied to his own questionnaire that his Edenic religion would be "Roman Catholic in an easygoing Mediterranean sort of way," with "lots of local saints." This domesticated vision of a community that agrees on the requirements for sainthood, and agrees on them often and liberally, constitutes for Auden the religious example of the way in which a generalization might function in his own poetry. Declarations of value that assume widespread agreement become increasingly prominent as Auden's career progresses, but they must be examined within the context in which they appear because it is there amid the pedestrian details of his verse that his pronouncements and judgments take their familiar shape. The opening lines of Part Two of "New Year Letter" recall the younger, more apocalyptic Auden, sounding once again the ominous note of misdirection and mystery that had characterized an early lyric such as "The Watershed":

> Tonight a scrambling decade ends,
> And strangers, enemies and friends
> Stand once more puzzled underneath
> The signpost on the barren heath
> Where the rough mountain track divides
> To silent valleys on all sides,
> Endeavouring to decipher what
> Is written on it but cannot,
> Nor guess in what direction lies
> The overhanging precipice.

Here is a Dantean world of fated decisions, some of which will be profitable ones, some of which will lead to ruin, but all of which are made with little sense of well-being and integrity. An "estranged condition" hovers

over these lines, as Edward Mendelson in *Early Auden* has said of the earlier poem, and this, he argues, is "the true Auden country." But in "New
Year Letter," this vignette is followed by several lines that suddenly
transpose the narrator's perspective from the ground-level, "barren
heath" of Auden's true country to another plane altogether, one from
which *ex cathedra* statements seem ordained by the fluency of the verse
that delivers them:

> How hard it is to set aside
> Terror, concupiscence and pride,
> Learn who and where and how we are,
> The children of a modest star,
> Frail, backward, clinging to the granite
> Skirts of a sensible old planet. . . .

As a response to the dire geography that precedes this section, these
somber confessions might elicit sympathy from us for Jarrell's charge of
interminable moralizing. The opening of Part Two, the argument would
go, re-creates a moment that has become typical in twentieth-century literature, the moment of chronological disjunction when the narrator or
main character begins to realize that his or her own sense of time, or history, has fallen out of joint with a newly arrived chronological order. The
misperception normally creates the characteristic anxiety of the work.
Examples: the little boy in James Joyce's "Araby" who is caught in the
bazaar as it is closing and its lights are being extinguished; the narrator of
W. B. Yeat's "The Second Coming" who seems confident that "some
revelation is at hand"; or April in "The Waste Land," Eliot's "cruelest
month." In much twentieth-century writing, it is always later than we
think. Auden's version naturally lacks Yeats's prophetic grandeur and
Eliot's urbane desperation, and it is not meant to carry the plotted sub-
tlety of Joyce's fictional narrative, but it encapsulates the one technique
that we recognize as being essentially Audenesque: the simultaneously
clear and oblique depiction of a landscape, which forces on us ultimately
the recognition that here is the landscape of psychological motivation, or
to use the jargon, a psychologized landscape. Why then, having suc-
ceeded in this substantial depiction of the mind of Europe on the verge of

war, would Auden resort to the rhetorical posturing that follows: "How
hard it is to set aside / Terror, concupiscence and pride"? Or so Jarrell, in
a benevolent mood, might have wondered.

The answer lies in Auden's developing theory of poetry, the latter
stages of which Lucy McDiarmid in her recent book, *Auden's Apologies for
Poetry*, has done much to elucidate. McDiarmid argues that after 1939 –
the date is of course approximate – Auden began to abandon his earlier,
socially committed notion that poetry might serve as a vital criticism of
society, a criticism that would result ultimately in reformation. Early on,
Auden seems even to have dreamed of poetry as acknowledged legisla-
tion – this perhaps was one of his earliest corrections of Romantic doc-
trine – but as his career progressed, McDiarmid argues, his major poems
began to function as a type of "*retractio*, a statement of art's frivolity, vanity, and guilt." Accordingly, the voice that animates most of these poems
insistently sounds the note of apology, deprecation, and humility. So, to
answer Jarrell's charge that Auden endlessly moralizes, McDiarmid most
likely would respond that such moralizing represented Auden's attempt
to write poetry about poetry's impotence – a kind of verse that naturally
entails analytical commentary and the attendant abstract language.

But I would recast McDiarmid's central, helpful observation concerning Auden's growing diffidence when confronted with the question of
art's ultimate social value. Over the past decade, most of Auden's critics,
as well as the biographer Humphrey Carpenter, have mentioned Auden's
return to the church; indeed, Carpenter titles one of his chapters
"Conversion," and McDiarmid cogently excerpts a passage from one
of Auden's untitled essays, depicting his serious engagement with the
question of absolute value: "If, as I am convinced," Auden wrote, "the
Nazis are wrong, and we are right, what is it that validates our values and
invalidates theirs?" McDiarmid goes on to say that Auden spent the rest
of his career advocating the position that poetry, as a human, fallible, cultural artifact, was incapable of providing these absolute truths, the ones
needed for validation. "Culture is one of Caesar's things," Auden wrote
in "Postscript: Christianity and Art."

Reading the verse in question, however, I am as uncomfortable with
Auden's dismissals as I am with McDiarmid's confirmation of those dismissals. Auden's developing poetic theory was always aware of Caesar's
general ownership of culture, a Christian perspective, to be sure. Accord-

ing to Auden, absolute values, to the degree that they are ever made manifest to the human community, simply did not belong in poetry, or any other art for that matter. Caesar, from Auden's perspective, finishes second to God, but second place in that contest would be considered by any of its willing participants to be a worthy and ordained showing. Although McDiarmid claims that poetry for Auden could never "provide absolutes," it does not follow that his poetry could not attempt a prolegomenon, so to speak, to the future of an absolute value. When McDiarmid continues by claiming that Auden's later poetry represents "a poetics of apology and self-deprecation, a radical undermining of poetry itself," I would qualify this statement by adding that as Auden undermined one theory of poetry that had established itself as the primary mode of poetic expression, he instituted another theory – incompatible with much twentieth-century aesthetics – that viewed poetry as an art adjunctive to a supremely important ethical argument. But this is hardly to undermine poetry itself; it is only to undermine a dominant notion of poetry.

So I feel, in fact, that we have not taken Auden's dismissals seriously enough because we have not yet determined just what sort of poetry he offers as a replacement. The vast upheavals that occurred in poetic theory toward the end of the eighteenth century have caused, among many other things, a disenfranchisement of the couplet from the contemporary idiom.

Yet Auden not only wrote couplets seriously – many serious poets have regrettably done so – Auden wrote them well and with credible vigor. Pope would have been as uncomfortable in Auden's "true country" as Auden had been incapable of embodying Pope's Augustan rectitude, but the aphoristic couplets that seem standard fare in Pope – the ones, perhaps, that moralize interminably? – appear in Auden's poetry too, but with a variation: they are most often set in close proximity to the various versions of Auden's country that appeared throughout his career. Two clashing sensibilities, that of the eighteenth and twentieth centuries, are thus yoked together. In the following passage, Auden begins with the kind of particular, individuating description that twentieth-century poetry has enshrined, but toward the end of the passage, he reveals the typical direction of his thought as it moves from specific example to encompassing category:

> No matter where, or whom I meet,
> Shop-gazing in a Paris street,
> Bumping through Iceland in a bus,
> At teas where clubwomen discuss
> The latest Federation Plan,
> In Pullman washrooms, man to man,
> Hearing how circumstance has vexed
> A broker who is oversexed,
> In houses where they do not drink,
> Whenever I begin to think
> About the human creature we
> Must nurse to sense and decency,
> An English area comes to mind,
> I see the nature of my kind
> As a locality I love,
> Those limestone moors that stretch from Brough
> To Hexham and the Roman Wall,
> There is my symbol of us all.

The last line, "There is my symbol of us all," represents the one most hostile to the contemporary sensibility, the one so deeply fearful of the various discriminations that empower the dominant discourses of our culture. As a declarative statement, the line assumes a kind of human commonwealth and depends on what historians of psychology refer to as an essentialist theory of personality – all people, of whatever sexual preference, from whatever era or economic strata, share certain essential characteristics beyond the need for physical sustenance. Common sense makes it seem likely that we could hold long fruitful discussions with Cleopatra, but much recent theory on this matter assures us that our difficulties in doing so would be formidable. Yet Auden, although aware of the ways in which notions of historical continuity are often fabricated by a culture's powerful elite, comments on the particular bond that he has formed with the limestone landscape, and again we hear the generalizing, almost didactic tone that seems determined to find such continuity in his own life:

> But such a bond is not an Ought
> Only a given mode of thought,

Whence my imperatives were taught.
Now in that other world I stand
Of fully alienated land,
An earth made common by the means
Of hunger, money, and machines,
Where each determined nature must
Regard that nature as a trust
That, being chosen, he must choose,
Determined to become of use. . . .

In this "fully alienated land," Auden is "determined to become of use," determined to participate in what he considered our birthright as human beings – those "loose formations of good cheer," as he phrased it, "Love, language, loneliness and fear." But he insisted on pursuing his investigations of these loves and fears to the point of considering their absolute values, considering their potential to support general statements concerning our plight, and as he did so, he wrestled with the difficulty that confronts all contemporary ethicists. The simple fact of moral diversity, the lack of common foundational principles that all communities are bound to accept as justified, leads to the kind of moral relativity that Auden abhorred, but his inability to locate through his art a transcultural source of value made his abhorrence seem impractical, or even worse, immodest.

He ultimately relegated this latter worry, of course, to his faith, but he could never remove the vestiges of this concern from his poetry. And I think he never wanted to do so, even though he could ask, "Is there not something a little odd, to say the least, about making an admirable public object out of one's feelings of guilt and penitence before God?" It never bothered Donne or Hopkins to create such objects, and Auden confessed that these poets always made him uneasy. But Auden has created – and I take it to be the signal achievement of his later verse – a verbal topography littered with fragments of ethical arguments, with isolated phrases, seemingly abandoned generalizations, the word-hoard, in short, of a poet who inherited Eliot's vocabulary of psychic fragmentation and is attempting to construct, without entirely abandoning our century's idiom, a poetic language adequate to his ethical sensibility. In "New Year Letter," Auden speaks of the small community gathered together in Mayer's

house and describes it as being unified by "a common meditative norm /
Retrenchment, Sacrifice, Reform." Although these were the war years in
which such values were advertised to the point of sloganeering, Auden
saw this "meditative norm" as standing at the center of his sense of community. The poet who seems destined to be remembered as the one who
thought poetry could make nothing happen continued by declaring art
the organizing agent of his own sense of communal order, his "local understanding": "For art had set in order sense / And feeling and intelligence, / And from its ideal order grew / Our local understanding too."
The various ideals that often structure artistic expression and remain so
intractable to social application have become, in fact, the agents of
Auden's "local understanding."

But how do we recognize and describe the literary form of an ethical
argument in the poetry? As I have indicated, Auden's verse marshals its
generalizations within contexts that are sharply specified. He makes it
very clear, for example, that the limestone moors of England exist as *his*
psychic reference point, and not ours, but he continues with his frank
confession that, like it or not, the limestone moors are for him, "the
symbol of us all." Auden's verse continually follows this pattern of con-
structing a particularized narration that is periodically interrupted by a
generalization of one sort or another, and these interrupting generalities
represent Auden's apparently unconquerable will to assess the value of
his material. His generalizations, as do all generalizations, presume to
ignore the individual needs or demands of race, culture, creed, gender,
and nationality, and they do so for a very simple reason: Auden believed,
and his verse shows, that doubts about the criteria propounded for a
moral truth do not necessarily constitute doubts about the existence of
moral truth.

Auden's poetic idiom, then, assembles and amalgamates the various
vocabularies descending to him from the tradition of ethical debate that
has characterized the century. These vocabularies are laden with skepticism, and sureties are purchased at a high price, but through his stubborn
willingness to coax the general statement from the debunking evidence
of his contemporary culture, evidence that clutters his poems, Auden
represented in his work the often exhausting give-and-take of such
debate. He used what he had at hand to portray the interruptive discon-

tinuities of human life, its "love, language, loneliness and fear," but somewhere along the way Auden decided not to stop with the evocation of those powerful sentiments; he decided to weigh them, to evaluate them, and thereby represent our equally human need for certainty and pronouncement. Auden's verse often seems composed by what Claude Levi-Strauss called a *"bricoleur,"* someone who "works with his hands and . . . with a set of tools and materials which is always finite and is also heterogenous [and] is the contingent result . . . of previous constructions or destructions." Continually juxtaposed in Auden's verse are strikingly contemporary modes of description confronted with fragments of monarchical austerity and presumption. It is, in Auden's hands, a method of argument in poetry that resembles the fundamental structure of a variety of ethical argument that Stout labels "moral *bricolage,*" and one that seems perfectly fitted to our current obsession with cultural diversity:

> All great works of creative ethical thought . . . involve moral *bricolage.* They start off by taking stock of problems that need solving and available conceptual resources for solving them. Then they proceed by taking apart, putting together, reordering, weighing, weeding out, and filling in. Recent moral philosophy tends to favor a particular kind of *bricolage* – the kind that draws sharp lines around a secularized moral language, dismissing all else as inessential. . . .

These sharp lines have now fortified this "secularized moral language" to the point that it seems nearly unassailable from any camp except that of the theologians, but the lines of communication between those two powerful persuasions have lain for at least two centuries in disrepair.

As Auden's career progressed, then, he increasingly turned away from the poetry of individuation that was the legacy of the Romantic and modernist writers. Yet this model still dominates most contemporary verse, urging us to celebrate ourselves, particularly in the first person, and particularly those aspects of ourselves that, for one reason or another, we deem unique and authentic. Most of our best verse is written in the singular first person. Auden, on the other hand, often seems determined to pursue a language that lies beyond that circumscribed by the powerful rhetoric of a secular ethics. But as we have seen, he chose to do so without resorting to the immodest flagellations of devotional verse. The resulting assemblage – avuncular, feisty, coherent – has not been accurately heard because it departs so surreptitiously from the mode of writing that dominates our era.

But it is, I believe, a substantial departure. Entirely typical of Auden's autumnal aesthetic is a long poem from the 1960s entitled "Thanksgiving for a Habitat." In a decade that had seen the solidification of such turbulent talents as Ginsberg, Lowell, Berryman, Sexton, and Plath, those arbiters of one stream of the contemporary idiom, Auden decided that his proper task would be to write a poem to every room in his house and to thank them for the life they each had encouraged and fostered. But it is not entirely an encomiastic poem. Part of Auden's growing problem concerned his subject matters, his ability to locate objects for common examination in a world where, as Stout has argued, "we have so little sense of common purpose in part because we have become so accustomed to a picture that hides the actual extent of our commonality from view." The rooms of a house, its kitchen, its bedroom, its bathroom, must have seemed for him an ideal forum, the physical embodiment of an ethical structure that practically every living human being had experienced first-hand and held in common ("Grub First, Then Ethics," he titled his poem to the kitchen). Yet in the Prologue to the poem, whose subject is the birth of architecture, Auden laments the demise of sacred structures and the integrated community that their naves, buttresses, and arches once reflected. Looking out of his window, he is never quite pleased with what he sees:

> . . . Among its populations
>   are masons and carpenters
> who build the most exquisite shelters and safes,
>   but no architects, any more
> than there are heretics or bounders: to take
>   umbrage at death, to construct
> a second nature of tomb and temple, lives
>   must know the meaning of *If*.

I take the grandly concluding "*If*" to descend from its purely grammatical sense of condition, but by extension to gather under its aegis those who would confront both the conditional nature of their lives and their abiding need for unconditional values, a need that often arises from despair. That we will "accomplish our corpse," as Auden once phrased it, certainly unites us all. How we respond to this fact often divides us. But the vast and clarified divisions that constitute our culture are not ameliorated, and should not fear amelioration, by encouraging the most difficult kind of dialogue, that which asks us to abandon, if only for the moment, our hard-won autonomies, and to do this for the purpose of pondering the influence that the search for foundational principles continues to exert on us. Auden attempted honestly to represent the difficulties of these dialogues in his verse, paying homage to every fallibility he encountered, yet responding to them with corrective vigor. For poetry makes nothing happen? It survives. A way of happening. A mouth.

DONALD JUSTICE

Oblivion: Variations on a Theme

[WESLEYAN WRITERS' WORKSHOP]

At a certain point in life, usually during adolescence, the artist dedicates himself or herself to art. I have a romantic view of this moment, which may overtake us unawares. It may be that the moment will already have passed before we quite know what has occurred; by then it may be too late to do anything about it. Nor will the artist feel it improper to speak, as is often done, in a language bearing overtones of the spiritual. It *is* a vocation. The vows may not be codified and published, but they are secretly known and one does take them. I am perfectly serious about this. Years later the significance, the great emotion involved in this commitment, may prove difficult to recall, and especially hard to keep in mind during the excitations and fluctuations of a career, the temporary successes and, if one is lucky, the only temporary failures. It may be hard also for outsiders not to be skeptical of the depth and force of the dedication when they overhear the chatter of novelists concerning the large sums of money coming to them or of poets concerning the inflated reputations of their rivals. It may be that we become like the priests in the stories of J. F. Powers, so much taken up with affairs of the Parish that the high moment of original dedication seems a contradiction. But for some of us it is always there, if only as a nagging whisper or the twinge and throb of guilt. We are aware of this dedication within ourselves, though at times embarrassed to acknowledge it. Others, of course, boast of it. More mysteriously, I believe we can spot such a dedication in others. I myself have seen it in others at an early age. All the same, it happens to be no predictor of success. What I am speaking of is something more inward, something invisible, rather like the self-satisfaction of the elect in certain Protestant sects.

Some dim notion of all this must underlie the critic's familiar envy.

Experience teaches one to believe that there is a dimension to the self that all those who are not artists lack; I believe it myself. There is a mysterious and hidden consciousness within the artist of being *other;* there is an awareness of some reality-beyond-the-reality that lures and charges the spirit; it charges and gives power to one's very life. Nor can it be easily forsworn in moments of agony or despair. If it does go, it is more likely to be dribbled away unobserved and piecemeal, buried eventually under a growing heap of dollars or blinked away in the brilliance of spotlight and starshine. Rejection, the success of inferiors, the scorn of reviewers – all these can beat and hammer one down; one may stop writing or painting for years, perhaps forever; it does happen, though more rarely than seems altogether reasonable. One of the most dedicated artists I have known – I will say more about him later – published in all his life fewer than half a dozen poems, not many more than Emily Dickinson or Gerard Manley Hopkins. As long as I knew him he never lost sight of the ideal I am trying to suggest; for him the light of this ideal rarely even flickered; it burned steadily. Whether this was a tragedy or a triumph I cannot say with confidence.

For many writers there comes also a second critical and perhaps overwhelming moment. In *The Literary Situation* Malcolm Cowley describes it this way:

> It's a good life. . . . But it has some bad years in it, especially around the age of forty. That's the time when writers have to face up to what they've been doing. . . . They are halfway through their artistic careers, and perhaps they've made a little success, but not the sort they were hoping for, and now the future begins to look like the past and not so interesting. They begin to wish desperately that everything could be changed, starting tomorrow – wives, jobs, friends, places, everything, before the walls close in.

Of course it can happen in much the same way to other artists besides writers. The abstract expressionist turns suddenly to realism; or vice versa. I take it that, looked at in the best light, this is not primarily a crisis of the practical; further, that it may be only coincidentally and peripherally connected with the midlife crisis many who are not artists likewise suffer. I understand it as a crisis involving the pursuit of the ideal with which one as an artist began. The ideal has proved elusive; now one begins to see that it will always be so. To argue that the very pursuit has somehow become the ideal to which one dedicated oneself is hardly adequate; it may be true, in its way, but that was not the language of the original contract, whether with the gods or the devil. This is the point at which the writer may stop writing altogether, at least for a while; or gradually write less and less, or less and less well; or drink a great deal more than is good for him; or jump off a bridge; or simply continue going through the motions he has grown used to, but with less and less joy. Whether this is somehow a prevision of the slide or plunge into oblivions that await virtually everyone, and of which artists are painfully conscious, I am not certain, but it may well be. The pull and drag toward oblivion is felt; it is set like the hook. This is the moment, let us suppose, when Ralph Hodgson, the English poet of more than one charming anthology piece, vanished from the public eye; years later he was to turn up, I seem to remember, on a farm in Ohio. One understands and can sympathize. Do such moves not resemble the fugues of the disturbed? There is a sorrow deep down at the heart of things, we would, many of us, agree; for the artist some sense of disappointment and frustration, some rage for and at the absolute, seems inevitable. Persistence in the face of such certitude of oblivion is in its small way heroic, or so my romantic spirit commands me to believe.

I come now to three examples from among the poets. Two were friends of mine; I edited the poems of the third. Together they show something of what recent literary culture has been. I do not mean the culture represented by the Mailers and the Ginsbergs, the tip of the crazy, tilted iceberg, but rather the one represented by other artists, far less visible, but true artists nonetheless. The news magazines and the academic establishment on which we so heavily depend for our opinions simply have no organs for seeing this underworld or underclass of art. Do not mistake me. I do not have in mind the productions of societies of amateurs, literary clubs, workshops; I mean the real thing. There may well be analyzable causes behind the oblivion some good writers suffer, but the causes, whatever they are, remain elusive. There is a randomness in the operation of the laws of fame that approaches the chaotic, and I believe that the various degrees of oblivion to which these three poets have been consigned are no more proportionate to the real value of their work than the fame of some others is to the value of theirs. The success of these three – what there was of it – ought to be measured in terms of the poems they wrote or perhaps by no more than a splendid phrase here or there, almost lost now. It may help to remember that underlying all this was the almost spiritual type of dedication I have been trying to identify. It is too dismal to concede that success is measured only in terms of notoriety and riches and such toys.

The first poet I would call to mind is Weldon Kees. Kees may by now have become something of a cult figure, though the cult is small. In claiming even this much I may be guilty of exaggeration, for as the editor of his poems I hear about most of whatever Kees activity there is and may therefore have a false picture of its extent. I can report within the last few years these signs of interest: a small exhibition of his paintings and collages on the West Coast; the publication, most belatedly, of a satiric novel rejected by Knopf during World War II; and, most curiously, a sort of celebration organized several years ago in his hometown of Beatrice, Nebraska, by an enterprising local high school teacher, which involved reminiscences by some who had known him as a youth, a couple of tour buses, several high school musicians, and so on. Fame of a sort, all this; at the same time, perfect subject matter for the missing author's own satiric eye. Whatever interest does still exist in Kees can be traced in part to the circumstances of his life, as must often be the case. Kees disappeared in July, 1955, and there have since that time been no reliable reports of his being seen, though I get rumors of sightings from time to time. (Recently a singer who knew him told me she had run into him two years after the disappearance in a beer parlor on Fair Oaks Avenue in South Pasadena. Oddly enough, they had exchanged no words, only a significant look.) Kees's car had been found abandoned in a parking lot adjoining the Golden Gate Bridge, but the body was never found. Although he had been urging a friend to flee with him to Mexico and start a new life, the assumption must be that he jumped. To some of the aura surrounding his last days I myself, in the introduction to his collected poems, must have contributed. I claimed that "if the whole of [Kees's] poetry can be read as a denial of the values of the present civilization, then [his] disappearance . . . becomes as symbolic an act as Rimbaud's flight or Crane's suicide." It may in truth carry some symbolic value – more perhaps than either Rimbaud's dramatic flight or Crane's more definitive leap – but it has not been taken as such by those outside Kees's circle of admirers.

Dana Gioia, one of those admirers, puts the case this way:

> By most . . . standards Kees is a forgotten writer. His work was ignored by anthologists during his life and even now is usually represented by two or three poems, if at all. Most anthologists ignore him altogether. . . . It may seem petty to bicker about his representation in anthologies until one remembers that the total printing of Kees's three books of poetry during his lifetime did not greatly exceed one thousand copies, and subsequent printings of his *Collected Poems* have not been much larger. If he were to have reached a larger audience, it would have been through anthologies. Even the one collection of his work currently in print has never been widely distributed.

In 1982 the paperback edition of his poems was allowed to lapse by the University of Nebraska Press. Itself an obscure press, it had been the publisher chosen by the poet's father, because of the Nebraska connection. This press of late has gone in for heavily designed, obviously costly publications, a huge Derrida, for instance, or a collection of statements about Paul de Man's collaborationist journalism, hot and trendy stuff, to be sure. This may explain the reply I had to a question about bringing the paperback version of the collected Kees back into print:

> At present, tight fiscal policy at our university requires that all paperback books we publish support their own publication costs. To do so, such books must sell about 1000 copies per year. Unfortunately, all the evidence we've seen indicates that the *Collected Poems* would not achieve that sales rate.

I asked about letting another publisher take over the book, but the director of the press, despite his own lack of interest, wanted some sort of payment, which his letter, as I read it, implied might amount to a considerable sum. If his estimate of the book's appeal is anywhere close to accurate, this would seem to be a contradiction: another publisher would be idiotic to pay for what can only lose money. What seems more indefensible to me: the copyrights should not be in the hands of anyone with this attitude; the only heirs remaining who have been traced are two or three distant cousins, I understand, who have no literary background but would seem more honorably entitled to whatever small fees the copyrights produce than a press this indifferent. (Although, to my great surprise, I received in the mail last week a paperback copy of a new printing of the Kees *Collected,* this without advance notice or any explanation for the publisher's change of heart.)

Admittedly, this is a relatively benign state of neglect or oblivion; but it *is* that, and it has required the efforts of several people to keep even this small flame alive. Here was a poet who, as Alfred Kazin remembered him forty years later, had "desperately wanted to be famous, to be 'up there,' as he used to say, with Eliot, Pound, and other stars in our firmament." A few years before his disappearance, Kees was to defend himself to his parents: "If you think it has been easy or without a struggle, or if you think it has all not been accompanied by the blackest kind of doubts and despair – or that many times I have wanted (but never for long) to chuck it all, you simply do not know." For such a mood, incidentally, this was his mother's remedy: "Egg nogs at least three times a day [to] give you strength. A few graham crackers with them." (One imagines the long hot summer afternoons of childhood in Beatrice, the boy secluded in his room reading away at Dostoyevsky, and the knock at the door: his mother bearing the tray on which rested the surefire Nebraska cure for the blues.) Another Kees letter from those last years: "I don't know what happened to my muse, but along the poetic front, things are quiet, very very quiet. Just not much of an impulse. Usual reaction to those I have is: 'I've been over this ground before.' Sometimes I incline toward the Scott Fitzgerald theory of emotional exhaustion, the idea that one has only so large an account to draw on, and once you've drawn on it, that's all there is. . . . I must say that these days I am frequently assailed with feelings that even efforts to produce art are both heartbreaking and absurd." A few writers may be spared, but in general these feelings are all too familiar to them. Kees himself went on to ask: "But what else is there?" – that is, besides art. This may be the question that holds the writer to his calling in the very face of oblivion. But for Kees, as it happened, it would not hold him forever.

Some time after the disappearance, a novelist friend of Kees's, by way of consoling the poet's parents, wrote them as follows:

The last time we saw him he was beside himself with rage and despondency—
about his future, his poetry, the state of the arts. . . . It was America that failed
him, really: our. . . outrageous and casual indifference toward anything which
makes a demand on our intelligence or reflection—. . . that was what his great
gentility of spirit and his moral sense could not endure.

Vague and grand all this may sound, but there *was* something beyond the
personal involved in the poet's feelings, and it cannot be wrong to locate
it, at least loosely, in the general culture.

But poetry is, in such a case, the best testimony in the case, and here is
one of the poems that people familiar with Kees's work know and identify it by.

ASPECTS OF ROBINSON

Robinson at cards at the Algonquin; a thin
Blue light comes down once more outside the blinds.
Gray men in overcoats are ghosts blown past the door.
The taxis streak the avenues with yellow, orange, and red.
This is Grand Central, Mr. Robinson.

Robinson on a roof above the Heights; the boats
Mourn like the lost. Water is slate, far down.
Through sounds of ice cubes dropped in glass, an osteopath,
Dressed for the links, describes an old Intourist tour.
—Here's where old Gibbons jumped from, Robinson.

Robinson walking the Park, admiring the elephant.
Robinson buying the *Tribune*, Robinson buying the *Times*. Robinson
Saying, "Hello. Yes, this is Robinson. Sunday
At five? I'd love to. Pretty well. And you?"
Robinson alone at Longchamps, staring at the wall.

Robinson afraid, drunk, sobbing. Robinson
In bed with a Mrs. Morse. Robinson at home;
Decisions: Toynbee or luminol? Where the sun
Shines, Robinson in flowered trunks, eyes toward
The breakers. Where the night ends, Robinson in East Side bars.

Robinson in Glen Plaid jacket, Scotch-grain shoes,
Black four-in-hand and oxford button-down,
The jeweled and silent watch that winds itself, the brief-
Case, covert topcoat, clothes for spring, all covering
His sad and usual heart, dry as a winter leaf.

I turn next to Henri Coulette. It is not that I view his work as a failure any more than I do Kees's; far from it. I think now, looking back, that there was a chance for him to have developed into a major poet; the times as they were and his temperament as it was did not cooperate to bring that about.

Shortly after Coulette's death in 1988, the poet Robert Dana remembered him this way:

Henri Coulette, Jane Cooper and I graduated during a record hot June in 1954 from the University of Iowa, where we had been members of Robert Lowell's and John Berryman's workshops. We had strong opinions about . . . a lot of things. And very high hopes. In some dilapidated album of mine there is a black-and-white photograph of the three of us on that day: Jane, who recently retired from her Sarah Lawrence post as a teacher of poetry, in the middle, Hank and I on either side. It's so hot and the sun so searingly bright and our shirts so white that they reflect the sunlight right back into the camera lens. At either side of Jane, our hair still cropped short in the military style of our respective theaters of World War II, Henri and I cast a blazing white aura. Lean (is "frail" a better word?), young Galahads eager to take on the world.

Coulette was to spend the rest of his life in his native California. It is a state full of marvels and an infinite variety, including poets, but if the kind of poetry most readers think of in connection with California is what a Bukowski or a Ferlinghetti or even a Levine might produce, that is not really the whole story. There is, beyond that, the elegant and cool example of Coulette's work.

In any case, he remained devoted to the special California he partly invented and partly was invented by. It pleased him to slip unobtrusively into one of his own poems a line stolen from LBG-30, an early Glendale computer programmed to write verses; to this LBG-30 he would sometimes refer as "the other poet" of southern California. The line is,

"Where flying woefully is like closing sweetly," and to me, an outlander, it seems somehow to be *about* California, as it is certainly about death. A brother had been a detective with the Los Angeles Police Department, a fact in which Coulette took pride. It allowed him the illusion of poking about in the mists of Hollywood history and speculating about matters like the famous unsolved murder in the twenties of the director William Desmond Taylor. His notebooks make it clear that for years he hoped to write a long poem dealing with the Taylor case, perhaps even solving it, for he told me once that his detective brother had come across official but secret papers that pointed to a solution never made public. He liked to visit the old Hollywood Cemetery, filled with monuments of film immortals – including the murdered Taylor, whose ashes reposed in a shallow sliding tray, as did Peter Lorre's and Rudolf Valentino's. I kept expecting poems, perhaps even a sort of comedy of the City of Angels, reflecting all this lore he delighted in. I would not have been greatly surprised if something along these lines had turned up among his boxes of papers, but very little did show. There was one small poem mentioning Brecht in his Hollywood days, another – unfinished – about Charlie Chaplin and his then young bride Oona shopping in the old Pickwick Bookshop, one of Coulette's favorite haunts. Here is one of the finished poems that did come out of Coulette's vision of Hollywood.

THE EXTRAS

Today, they are the subjects of a king,
And they must cheer his passage through the town
This coronation morning, cheer his taking
Purple and ermine, the scepter and the crown.

They have, they will again, take after take,
But now the star, his agent at his sleeve,
Has disappeared. Their thoughts come back to them
Like shadows, and they rest from make-believe.

Duchess and chimney sweep are Blossom and Hank.
A light is asked for, and a light is given.
Gossip is music played upon the breath
By wicked tongues, and anecdote is heaven.

Simply human is what their costumes smell of;
Simply human is what their faces say.
They make the lobby and the street look real.
Practicing every day for Judgment Day,

They draw the circle that becomes the crown;
They draw bathwater on a bended knee,
And curtains on the night, and they draw blood.
They are the after that comes After Me.

If there should truly prove to be such a trove as I have imagined – and it would not much surprise me to learn of one – it has yet to be discovered in any of the likely places. But with neglected writers such mysteries and losses are common; they constitute a part of the very definition of the type of oblivion we are dealing with. Think of the letters given over to flames and garbage dumps, the unsorted boxes of papers lying about in attics and basements, the notebooks scrawled in drunken, half-legible squiggles and codes, kept in fading ink, never to be deciphered. What glories, what banalities, what secrets!

Just as one of the older poets he admired, J. V. Cunningham, once called himself "a professional writer, however laconic, one to whom poetry was verse," so Coulette, with a defiant modesty that was altogether characteristic, considered himself "a *maker* rather than a *bard*. From this consideration," as he put it, "all else follows. I am interested in technique, and take pride in demonstrating it. . . . I like to think that I bear witness to experience; i.e., that my subject matter is being me, here, now. I hope that I may rise above these limitations, but I have no illusions about being a spokesman for others, or of possessing the truth. Limitation is a mystery, and I try to live with the excitements and discomforts thereof." He possessed a delicate and alert ear, grounded in the traditional meters but by no means restricted to them; and for poets whose work showed little or no interest in the rhythms of poetry – an increasing number, he believed – he had little sympathy. He felt perhaps most at ease in the syllabic meters, and the syllabic stanza he devised for the long title poem of his first book, *The War of the Secret Agents*, shows his mastery of the form. (In England he was to go to some trouble to meet Jean Overton Fuller, upon whose *Double Webs*, an account of the betrayal of a British spy network in World War II, his own angry, witty, and bittersweet poem was based. He reported afterwards his pleasure at having by a sort of occult intuition so exactly struck off, years before they met, the eccentric author's character in his own poem.)

He spent virtually his entire teaching life at Los Angeles State, where he had been an undergraduate. One remembers that as a bored and lonely child he had memorized the school colors of all the American colleges and how chagrined he was later when Philip Roth got the colors of Ohio State wrong in *Goodbye, Columbus* and did not care enough to correct the mistake. Coulette liked to get and have things right; and whatever of wildness may be thought obligatory in the lives of poets, a measure of which was undoubtedly present in his own makeup, he still wished to accommodate it to the sense of order he constantly desired, in life and in art. All in all, Coulette thought of himself as one who enjoyed the good life, and a part of the time he did, quietly, and in his own way:

> A one-eyed cat named Hathaway on my lap,
> A fire in the fireplace, and Schubert's 5th
> All silvery somewhere on a radio
> I barely hear, but hear – that is, I think
> As close as I may come to happiness.

His career had begun well enough. *The War of the Secret Agents*, his first book, was the Lamont Poetry Selection for 1965. But his second and last book, *The Family Goldschmitt* (1971), was, through a ridiculous error, shredded in Scribners' warehouse before it had much of a chance at distribution; so the author was told. This was a blow from which in a sense Coulette's reputation never recovered. The tide of opinion regarding American poetry in those years had begun to run, sometimes violently and with a very bad humor, against the very kind of poetry Coulette admired and most wished to write himself. Some neglect was probably inevitable, even destined. A part of the poet's defense was a cultivated silence, the silence of an exile from his own time, which in some ways he had chosen to become. He told his former student, the poet Michael Harper – "I don't know, Mike, I don't know whether we all got caught up in learning how to respond to having careers, or something of that sort. It's at that point that I started developing a terrible distrust of the whole world of the poets. . . . I think that we all got too caught up in dealing with that business, of being performers and having careers. We should have been better to each other." Four years before his death he put his concerns in a letter to me: "My depression finds all sorts of reasons for being. The deaths of friends, the deterioration of my college, of the profession. The awful sickness of poetry in our times. Do I mean sickness or silliness? I think back some 25 or 30 years to when poetry was something both noble and fun." The tune is not quite the Keesian tune, but the modulation into the minor is the same. Over and over this is the pattern; I have seen it more than once; there is nothing to be done.

Out of this near silence there did gradually accumulate over the years, in spite of everything, the poems for a third book, to which he was to add the last poem, "These United States," a poem about William Carlos Williams, only weeks before his death. He had time to make only one or two efforts to publish a version of this manuscript; one that I know of was rebuffed with a note the author rightly found patronizing but by which he was not at all surprised. Feeling that those last years had produced some of his finest work, I wrote, not long after his death, to an editor with whom I had a certain acquaintance. Here is a part of the well-meaning reply accompanying the return of the manuscript: "I've showed them [the poems] to some of the staff here and alas the word is no. . . . This is not because we're not doing poetry anymore. Rather, it's because the powers that be here want to publish people with a future – i.e., the newly established. We simply aren't in the market for poems from non-living authors." By such terms, which of us has a future? Is this oblivion? Not quite, perhaps. This third book of Coulette's is now included in the volume of *Collected Poems* brought out by the University of Arkansas Press a few years ago. It has been reviewed very well, if not broadly. In the end, of course, we must face the simple fact that most publication too is only a somewhat more benign form of oblivion, a variation on the theme, but it is about all that can be expected or even, perhaps, hoped for. There will be this much then, we say, as a record; there will be this trace.

I come now to the last and by far the most obscure of the three poets. Anyone who has not read my poems, and pretty thoroughly at that, is unlikely to have heard of Robert Boardman Vaughn. No one will now remember the two poems he published in *Poetry* more than twenty years ago, nor the old sestina he published in a long defunct literary magazine known as the *Western Review*. It is the only poem of his I have ever heard anyone mention who was not personally acquainted with him. I consider it quite a beautiful small piece of work; infinitely touching to me. About the circumstances of Vaughn's death – if he is dead – as little seems known as about Kees's.

In the first version of his death to reach me, back in the early seventies, Vaughn's body was said to have been found floating in Miami's Biscayne Bay, unidentified for days. This story surfaced at a party in Miami, the sort of party the poet himself, toward the end, might have wandered into, invited or not – sandals flapping, eye patch covering the one missing eye, caved-in chest. Later, I heard that he had been beaten to death in the hallway of a halfway house in Manhattan; later still, that the beating had taken place instead in an alley running alongside the halfway house. All versions were plausible enough, but I believed this last one. It was winter when I heard it, and I remembered those alleys from our early days together in the city. It was easy to picture such an alley with the cold winds barreling through, and patches of snow crusted between the knocked-over and spilling ash cans.

It was a scene that seemed fated. Years before, Vaughn had gone about campus reciting the last lines of Hart Crane's "Chaplinesque," in which the moon is described as making in lonely alleys "a grail of laughter of an empty ash can." It isn't that I believe the favorite verses of our youth come back to haunt us, but in these lines, for Vaughn, there may have been something prophetic, an omen.

Another passage he liked to quote in those days was the one Shelley had taken from Wordsworth for the preface to "Alastor": "The good die first, / And those whose hearts are dry as summer dust, / Burn to the socket." We went around for months declaring that the good die first, certain that we ourselves had only a few short years to live out our lives. This was quite absurd. It was the height of World War II, and we were among the handful of civilian males left on campus, both 4-F. Oddly, I don't think it occurred to us to connect Wordsworth's lines with the young men in the Navy V-12 program on campus, who might soon be in actual danger. The lines were noble and beautiful; probably we would not then have conceded that that was why we liked them. They confirmed our sense of belonging to an elect, though doomed. The future, what there might be of it, would be lived at the most intense level of sensation and in pursuit of the highest art. (Everyone will, I hope, remember something of that feeling.) A third favorite passage of Vaughn's he must have picked up from some freshman reader, a fragment of Robert Louis Stevenson: "condemned to some nobility." An unlikely phrase to apply to anyone who was to live a life as terrible and as terribly wasted as Vaughn was to do, but I have come around now to seeing his life that way, and I think Vaughn must have seen it that way from the start. Our touchstones had for him an almost scriptural authority.

Whoever knew Vaughn well, then or later, seemed automatically to assume that his life was emblematic. He did himself. He was Poet, Wanderer, Revolutionary. All his life he had a frail look, sometimes a hunted look, and no one expected him to live long. To pass the ripe age of forty, as he was to do, was a matter of luck and grace, not will, not probably in the end desire. His life was like the flight of an arrow aimed for oblivion. But aimed.

In an interview given in his late thirties to a local newspaper, Vaughn, who had already been at it for twenty years, with next to nothing to show for it, called writing poetry "a mania, almost . . . very demanding. Sometimes you drive yourself over the edge . . . I get used to listening to people say at my age I ought to get a steady job and a trade and get my feet on the ground. I'm not sure I want my feet on the ground." At the time he was temporarily helping his mother out in a small produce business in Miami. There was further wandering; no publication. A few years later he was writing a professor with whom a friend had stored some of Vaughn's goods: "Would you please mail or Railway Express my manuscript and notebooks (all the stuff that L. stored there) to me at Lexington. [At the time Lexington was the federal drying-out retreat for addicts.] I may be leaving soon and it's important that I have the material in order to prepare a book for publication." It was not to be. Twenty years before, there had been this, in a letter to a woman friend: "I've been trying to write and tonight, for the first time in many days, but few attempts, have written about 5 pages of original and economical prose. I am nervously contented." Moments like that, were they enough? Sentimentally, I like to think that they were, or very nearly were.

A few summers ago came this inquiry from a handpress printer I know. "I've been meaning to write you for some time. I was wondering if you have a Robert Boardman manuscript. I saw the two poems in your book and got the impression that there were more. Unfortunately I loaned the book out so I have to rely on memory." I wrote back to the effect that the name was Vaughn and that the poems, though about Vaughn, had been written by me. I would be happy, though, to send him a portion of a Vaughn manuscript to sample. This reply: "Thanks. . . . The Robert Boardman Vaughn manuscript is what I meant. Maybe you could send me some of it so I have an idea what I'm getting into." I did. This was four or five years ago now. No reply; silence; oblivion.

Yet there are fragments and stanzas possessing, if you have a taste for it, great beauty of a certain high romantic kind, poems of a piece with this wasted life of fragments. Whole poems have been lost, doubtless forever; and probably, in truth, it does not much matter. One from the Caribbean, a favorite subject of Vaughn's, was called "Pilgrim's Terrace"; the rhythms of this poem seemed a revelation to me at one time; now gone forever. Only my memory of the title remains. After this, who will ever mention it again?

In my possession is an incomplete manuscript that I have ransacked for passages to quote. If these passages now seem out of fashion, it is quite likely that they were never strictly *in* fashion. They belonged instead to what might be called a tradition made up by the poet himself – a Poundian assemblage – out of what he had once been impressed by and would always thereafter be loyal to; they reflect a personal and heroic taste.

From a poem to someone named Judith:

> Where you are is where the Rose
> Unfolds and brings an answer
> Men have watched for on the high
> Plateaus towards Everest.

Or the end of "The Last Letter to Ernesto Guevara":

> There, Magellanic ultramarine
> and I'll meet you out on the Gulf Stream
> with sailfish and white butterflies
> where there is no such thing as humanism in the abstract

but there is a bright lament always
and where is my dun-colored horse
unnamed till Santa Fe, those doors beyond
relentless gates, dead friend.

Or this, after meeting one time in Miami Beach the actor Lionel Stander, years later to become the butler of the TV series "Hart to Hart"; Stander had recently played a pipe-smoking, corduroy-jacketed sort of proletarian poet in the bizarre Ben Hecht movie, *The Specter of the Rose,* which must have appealed to Vaughn, who sometimes in those days smoked a pipe and wore an old green corduroy jacket himself:

So speak, Stander.
In the angles and corners of South Beach,
Propose your dialogues to a white resort.
For this is the time of our lives. Moonmist
And the stars are sparkling on abandoned screens.

Of Thomas Wolfe, an adolescent admiration:

Stuttering through syllables as one
Sleepwalks through fields of violets towards home.

Or, from his travels, a line I adapted in one of my poems about Vaughn:

the sight
Of torches by the railroad track in Medellín.

And, finally, the first two stanzas of the sestina referred to earlier; the first line is a quotation from a then-current Donald Hall sestina.

"Hang it all, Ezra Pound, there is only one sestina."
He read that by a window where the light
Recalled the lines he'd seen at Pisa. All
The words surrounded him again and death
Was silence. He'd forego that vanity
And work on cantos that he had not done.

There is an end to cantos when they're done
And Daniel once had written his sestina.
One cannot mind the young man's vanity.
They read beside the almost dead for light.
His lines would form their patterns after death,
The young are iron. The trick is singing all.

A few years ago, thinking of Dante's encounters with his dead friends
in hell and in purgatory, I put into my friend's mouth this speech:

After so many years of pursuing the ideal,
I came home. But I had caught sight of it.
You see it sometimes in the blue-silver wake
Of island schooners, bound for Anegada, say.
And it takes other forms. I saw it flickering once
In torches by the railroad tracks in Medellín.

When I was very young I thought that love would come
And seize and take me south and I would see the rose;
And that all ambiguities we knew would merge
Like orchids on a word. Say this:
I sought the immortal word.

Thinking then of other poets also, and particularly of Ser Brunetto in
Canto 15 of *The Inferno*, who, turning to join his troop of condemned fellow spirits, had seemed to Dante like one running in the race for the prize
of the green cloth at Verona, and who had seemed like one who wins, not
loses; thinking of all this, I added:

So saying he went on
To join those who preceded him;
and there were those that followed.

MARILYNNE ROBINSON

Hearing Silence: Western Myth Reconsidered

[IN THE THOREAU TRADITION]

I am the last person in the world to assume that words like "myth," or "Western," or "American" can be used with precision. Still, they have their place. I have spent a good deal of time reading about European history and institutions, and I am utterly convinced that the habit of speaking of American culture as if it were essentially continuous with European culture is a source of much error. The difference, I think, results from the great confluence of peoples that so particularly characterizes our history. Our forebears were for the most part not from the strata of society that embody official cultures, or whose manners, dialects, or sympathies would have been made rigid by the belief that they were pure, approved, or correct. There is no reason to expect such streams of influence to remain unmodified. One might expect them to combine and recombine, until their separate sources become untraceable. To speak as we now do of minority cultures seems to foster the assumption that the dominant culture is, in all significant respects, white and Northern European. I do not assume this. It seems to me ethnocentric if not ethnomaniacal to think one culture (as if turbulent Northern Europe could be called one culture) could smother out all competitors for influence. When one uses the word "American," one takes the risk of being understood in that narrow sense. The dangers of the word "Western" are the same. Tendentious definitions have the attraction of simplicity.

I know my use of these words is not systematic. But then, systems are most successful in dealing with problems that have been simplified to accommodate them. Language is not well adapted to reality. It becomes less so when its limitations are forgotten.

I consider myths to be complex narratives in which human cultures stabilize and encode their deepest ambivalences. They give a form to contradiction that has the appearance of resolution. When Greek gods favor or bully Greek heroes, free will and destiny interact as if they were more or less compatible. That is the point Socrates missed when he ridiculed the Homeric gods' behavior. He had little positive interest in free will or destiny, if it is fair to judge by *The Republic*. So the myths did not address an ambivalence that engaged him.

Myth is never plausible narrative. It asks for another kind of assent. To anyone for whom it does not strike an important equipoise, it seems absurd. The myth of the Fall makes it possible to think of humankind and the world as at the same time intrinsically good and intrinsically evil. Those to whom this vision is not compelling grumble about the apple and the snake.

I speculate that the attraction of the mind to myth comes from a sense that experience really is more complex than we can articulate by any ordinary means, or more than momentarily, emblematically. We know from physics that contrary things can be true at the same time, and we seem also to know this intuitively. I would suggest that the power of myth lies in the fact that it arrests ambivalence. I would suggest also that myths are coined continuously, usually in very small denominations, and that lesser myths are related to greater ones as a penny is related to a gold mine. Conceding all differences, they are describable in essentially similar terms. That is to say, I believe real myths appear and have their power, everywhere, even among us.

Contemporary cultures are put together out of all sorts of things – advertising campaigns, junk entertainment, the certitudes of the academies, machines with crude brains in them, floods of dubious information. We know we have not evolved as our material circumstances have elaborated themselves. We live like cargo cultists, among artifacts whose origins we could not begin to describe. Many of them seem to us to possess an uncanny value. Others we find ominous. We imagine we are passively conditioned by these things, dehumanized, but I think it is as likely that we prowl the landscape awestruck by the totems we have set up, sure that our wills are in the power of magicians, more or less in the manner of our remotest ancestors. The great joke of the human situation is that we do not know and can never know what the world is in itself, where it stops and we begin. I have read that American satellites did not pick up the hole in the ozone layer because their instruments are designed to discount extreme data. This seems to me to epitomize us, in a way. Americans consider it only reasonable to discard information that does not confirm their assumptions. This accounts for much of our peculiar immunity to experience and history, not to mention information itself. Our brilliant machines permit us to make characteristic mistakes on a grander scale. This is only to say that we are as trapped in our humanity as anyone ever was.

So it seems to me worth the experiment to say American myths work like other myths do by transforming ambivalence into a kind of equilibrium. My object is simply to set what we do back into a human context. It is only because we have deified our props and machines – cargo cultists that we are – that we can imagine our doings and thinkings are impinged upon by other than human forces.

The West was the last theater of the oldest ambivalence in American culture, from the point of view of the European settlement here. This is only to say that the West was an event in the life of the whole country, an astonishingly apt metaphor for a historic doubt as to the compatibility of freedom and civilization. That in itself made it certain to be the locus of powerful myth. I think we have now outlived that ambivalence, simply because neither freedom nor civilization continues to have much hold on our imagination. In our America the word "free" is likely to be followed by "trade" or "enterprise." We attribute this to the circumstances of our creation, on no grounds, except that if we can blame the Founders, what we do is excused and allowed, almost compelled. Jefferson foresaw this decline, grimly. But who, outside Prague, reads Jefferson?

It would be fortunate if we could provide, at this juncture in history, a conception of freedom somewhat more capacious and congenial to the human spirit, but all we seem to come up with is the map to a wilderness we have never crossed. If people persist long enough in paying money they do not have for sustenance they cannot find, at last they will be free. Stand in the street for four hours trying to sell a broken umbrella, and you, too, will taste the elixir of freedom. No wonder the newly liberated so readily pour their hopes into other vessels.

But freedom was once a beautiful idea, and so was civilization, and the dread associated with them both was not always strong enough to reduce the tension between them to our present dreary stalemate. The West as myth could not survive without that tension. To the very great extent that it was the work of the national and world imagination, it has not survived.

And of course there was and is a real West. I grew up in it, in lumber towns. Anything Western – pearl-button shirts, electric guitars, knotty-pine paneling, Morris couches with Indian blankets thrown over them – *any*thing Western seemed like raw provincialism. Once there was a school assembly for an old man who played a long, gleaming, tremulous saw with a fiddle bow. We were told we must listen closely, because it was becoming rare that one heard such a thing. But the old man was cross and distracted. He knew he did not have our attention. I remember the first sentence in the first history lesson to be presented to my dawning literacy: England is our mother country.

At my grandparents' ranch old men sat around the dinner table and laughed about disasters they had survived. Old dogs hunted in their sleep. Trout and venison, huckleberries, flour in talcy pillows, a gate on a chain weighted with a cowbell. A barn as silver as feathers lying along a hillside like a bird with a broken wing, the prettiest example I have ever seen of true Western ramshackle. Yet it seemed to me that everything I knew about the West I learned from the movies. The West was the hero of so many movies.

The West is where they make nuclear weapons and test them. I have read about the nuclear wastes being shipped into Idaho from the East Coast and from Taiwan, about British bombs exploded in Nevada. Anyone can interpret. The stuff is so dangerous only space and distance can isolate it, even provisionally. How convenient that there is the West to take the brunt of calamity. It is true of all the poorer and emptier places in the world that they have poverty to sell, and space, and also a political weakness that assures these commodities can be enjoyed by their purchasers without disruption. I have read that a Korean corporation has bought the right to log in Siberia, and that it is devastating great forests with marvelous efficiency, because no government in that part of the world can exert any control over it. Weakness and poverty can release a great deal of wealth, into a very few hands.

Perhaps it has become the economic role of the American West to be poor and empty, and also politically weak. The less economically tenable life in the West becomes, the more it is depopulated, the more it will be plundered. The suitability of a place for use as a toxic dump is inversely proportionate to the number of delegates it sends to Congress. The attractiveness of waste storage as an economic option varies directly with the level of poverty. The cost of exploitation of resources drops with the cost of wages, and with the political pressure brought against environmental standards in areas of poverty; therefore, the economic stimulus to exploitation rises as populations contract. I hear sometimes the idea that if the West could be largely depopulated, its environment could be restored. On the contrary, it will become more and more a province and a dependency, and it will suffer every abuse such regions suffer. If there is to be a West in any tolerable sense of the word, then there must be Westerners, that is, people who make lives here.

To the extent that the region was ever protected by associations with hope or heroism, there is little left to appeal to. We know now that the paintings that showed these mountains or these prairies bathed in theological light were not naïve but deluded; though they are, in fact, from time to time, bathed in what must resemble a theological light. Increasingly, the West is thought of as no more than the scene of a great crime, where the country's worst tendencies have had their freest expression. Perversely, the more aware we seem to be that this is a holy land to the Native Americans, the more inclined we are to view it and treat it as a desecrated place. I have read that the reservations are being offered money to accept nuclear waste, on the theory, I suppose, that a little more cynicism will never be noticed.

Most of what I have seen in the way of academic history of the West confirms these attitudes, as if it were doing something brave, going *against* a current. We all know that certain versions of history are urged upon us now, as if to take another view were to excuse the crimes of the past. It is salvation being preached—believe as I believe and your sins will be washed away. But look at the world we make: while we anatomize

General Custer yet again, tuberculosis and alcoholism, poverty and suicide hasten his old work of destruction, worse every day of *our* generation's ascendancy. If he were to come back among us, how would we prove to General Custer that his war had not resumed after a lull, and with smaller risk to his side than he would have considered honorable? We could tell him we now say "Native American." But it might take more than that to convince him.

We are merciless in our judgment of history – to the extent that what we talk about should be called history – but in many ways we do worse than the generations before us. It seems reasonable to me to wonder if we are misspending our energy. If the new version of history were truth, then it would be necessary to accept it, without raising questions about the motive behind its telling and the effect it will have on its hearers. But it is, transparently, myth, and so such questions are appropriate.

In 1801, Thomas Jefferson appealed to Congress to ease naturalization laws in these terms: "And shall we refuse the unhappy fugitives from distress that hospitality which the savages of the wilderness extended to our fathers arriving in this land? Shall oppressed humanity find no asylum on this globe?" This is myth, too. We know that many of the original European settlers were not fugitives, and that the indigenous people were not always hospitable. A Virginian would have been especially aware of this. Because his words have so little to do with fact, it is interesting to see what is established in Jefferson's narrative.

First, he wants the United States to be a land of refuge. His version of our origins establishes refuge-seeking as the quality Americans will have in common – not, say, religion or language, as would have been usual in the period. Compare J. G. Fichte's contemporaneous *Addresses to the German Nation*. Second, he makes the salutary point that the land does not really belong to the white settlers, even in anticipating and preparing for the arrival of more white settlers. Third, rather than representing the country as won through warfare from the indigenous people or from England, as a revolutionary leader might be expected to do, he tells his hearers that they are in America because of the graciousness of those to whom the land indeed belonged. Jefferson had great respect for Native Americans, and he was disturbed by the way they were being dealt with. At the same time, he thought of large-scale European immigration as a way of ending the labor shortage that made slavery viable, and he despised slavery. His myth creates an image of reconciliation among interests that would not be reconciled.

Our new and improved version of the myth of settlement has blond beasts with hegemony in their eyes indulging the appetites of conquest. Jefferson's refugees, with war or famine or persecution behind them, unvalued or unwelcome where they came from, have more to do with the truth, as events evolved. The immigration that followed 1848 was not a scheme to establish Irish dominance in the New World. It was without question the policy of the American government to settle the territories with farmers, to put an end to the prewar struggles for territory and influence between North and South that had led, as Lincoln argued, to the Mexican War. Lincoln, Marx, Harriet Beecher Stowe and others remarked on the powerful sympathy of European working people for the cause of the North. Their immigration was ideally suited to finally suppressing the slave economy and stabilizing the government. And it is remarkable, the degree to which the Civil War did come to an end, and a great savings in blood and sorrow. On the other hand, the settlement policy led to the brutal dispossession of the indigenous population. It was a situation in which, one way or another, injury would be suffered, wrong would be done.

The new version of the story of settlement sounds like some musty old race myth about exultant Aryans sweeping down from the steppes. There are more than a few people who would rather imagine themselves descended from an army of all-conquering Europe than from a swarm of folk desperate for work or a plot of ground or a change of luck. But we know as a matter of common sense that there is no truth in that story, and we should be grateful on esthetic grounds that there is not. A myth of origins serves to characterize a culture. It is arrived at by projecting backward from some present time, some present regime or enthusiasm that wishes to authorize or stabilize itself with the implication that it is inevitable. Origins are "discovered" in the collective memory or lore, as the moment in which the nature of the society can first be glimpsed. Caesar Augustus commissioned the *Aeneid*. Americans chose Plymouth rather than Jamestown as the settlers' definitive moment of contact with the New World—and this is interesting in light of the great influence of Virginians in the early period. If we say now that our origins were simply, merely, brutal, does that mean we assume we must always be brutal? Does it excuse us from other expectations? Do we want to be excused? Why else have we contrived this myth? Do we not assume, in other contexts, that the image we give people of themselves will affect their behavior? This Wagnerian drama of hegemony is powerfully, arbitrarily, associated with the West, and it has stigmatized the West, to the benefit of nothing and no one.

Reading James Galvin's book *The Meadow*, I was movingly reminded of the West of my memory. It occurred to me how intrinsic a part silence is of Western culture and experience, and how vulnerable they are to misinterpretation for that reason. It is truer of silence than of any speech, that if you do not understand it, no one can explain it. In this silence, I think, something of the old esthetic of freedom survives, something of the old individualism.

It seems to me Westerners subscribe to the notion of another order of goodness, one that consists largely in resisting the most available definitions of goodness. It seems to me they wish to proceed from an individual ethic rather than a social norm, to be self-consistent rather than merely reliable. I think they seek space and latitude through strategies of indirection.

I would suggest furthermore that fecklessness of a kind is built into the Western personality, as a form of moral and physical courage. It is a nod to human frailty, without which, after all, courage would be meaningless. And it is the sign and seal of a kind of orneriness that recognizes in self-interest yet another form of coercion. I would venture to say, too, that Westerners are quietists by nature. In some large part, they are descended from self-exiled people, who dealt with their quarrels with society by walking away from them. So they are less inclined than others to look to society for guidance or remedy. I think they tend to consider the brain an organ of delectation. They are of all people most likely to know things to which aesthetic pleasures attach, things to do with geology, astronomy, the ways of animals. Southerners are unsurpassed for humor and anecdote, but Westerners beat anyone at the remarkable, and they own the style of serious pleasure in which they confide it.

If this sounds like a version of Western myth, the Westerner as stoic Anglo-Saxon, then let us look at that word "Anglo-Saxon." In a context like this one it is a charged word, an indictment. We spend an enormous amount of time saying American culture is richly compounded of a great variety of cultures, and then we go on to speak of it collectively as a great dull fool with hardly a human trait. Obviously both these things cannot be true at once. So we are back again in the regions of myth. This supposed dullness and rapacity are laid to the charge of a dominant culture that is called "Anglo-Saxon." It would certainly be more precise to call it English or British, since Anglo-Saxons, descendants of the immigration from Germany, are only one demographic band of the British population and the British settlement here. For example, Jeffersons's origins were Welsh, not Anglo-Saxon.

But we admire the British for just those traits we find absent or repugnant in the "Anglo-Saxon." We think the British are stoical, yes, but also modest and mild and decent and tolerant and immune to materialism. So what an embarrassment it would be to call the dominant culture "English," although it would be, historically, less inexact. The phrase "Anglo-Saxon" is, in effect, an invention, an identity no one has to claim. If the function of myth is to encode ambivalence, to allow a culture to maintain at least two incompatible ideas in some sort of stable relation with each other, then this is probably a good example of myth. Americans are still so profoundly in awe of what they take to be their cultural origins that they cannot really criticize them, and must create a sort of dummy to absorb their resentments. The myth of the Anglo-Saxon pretends to revile what it, in fact, protects, which is the culture we take to have made the first and deepest impression on us. So once again, moral and critical energy is expended without result, and that may be the point. Myth seems inclined to promote stasis.

Let us consider that strange icon, the cowboy. To a degree that is striking in a society as nontraditional as this one, his appearance alludes to his history. He is surely remarkable as a male image in American culture in that he is permitted outright ornamentation, without utility or politeness to excuse it. He can wear bracelets, buckles and boots as intricate as court finery, and shirts embroidered with flowers. Nineteenth-century French writers remark on the *"dandyisme"* of the Indians, how beautifully their braves and great men attired themselves. Certainly Mexicans seem much more at ease with male adornment than Northern Europeans. The ranch, the rodeo, the lariat—clearly influence from that side was vast. So perhaps, as icon, "Anglo-Saxon" is precisely what the cowboy is not. Perhaps he represents a unique cultural syncretism, and is the true inheritor of just those influences whose suppression we all regret. Maybe we do well to like the look of him.

I note that so great an authority as John Wesley Hardin observes a distinction between cowboys and cowmen. This is a kind of distinction much older than this culture. Laborers were spoken of or to as children, employers as adults, everywhere in Europe. The word "cowboy" signified a very degraded kind of worker, a child, or an adult good for nothing else, who followed a cow all day, making sure it grazed where it should. Needless to say, "cowgirl" is equally venerable.

In the West, the cowboy acquired a horse and a weapon, traditional accoutrements of the privileged classes. He became associated with space and movement, his life resembling the lives of the indigenous people who followed the buffalo. It is interesting that it is the cowboy and not the cowman who became the world's hero, since he never ceased to be, in the economic terms of his time, an itinerant, a casual laborer. Karl Marx, his older contemporary, ponders the use of the word "hands" to describe factory workers, saying the term indicates the degree to which their humanity was denied. "Ranch hand" is as free of stigma as "cowboy."

What if the cowboy is the image of the worker in glory? What if his rise coincided with the rise of democracy, not accidentally, but because for the first time, and also the last time, the imagination of the world found the lives of such men worth mythifying and romanticizing? What if the new contempt in which we hold him empties the myth of its positive value because we participate in the abandonment of democracy as an ideal? What if we have remade him as an agent of capitalist hegemony because we cannot believe people ever did admire propertyless men who sold life and limb for a dollar a day?

Oh, I know, the cowboy is male. But in the time of this flourishing there were women, like Elizabeth Barrett, Harriet Beecher Stowe, and Jane Addams, who enjoyed influence and respect vastly greater than we now concede to any woman, dead or living. The absence of the female hero is our doing, not his.

The cowboy is associated with violence. So is the dragon. Heroics in every culture tend to revolve around episodes of violence, so one must exercise caution in drawing conclusions. The cowboy emerged after the Civil War, when there were hundreds of thousands of young men in the country not unaccustomed to shooting at other young men. It seems very probable that levels of violence would have been higher everywhere, simply as a psychological consequence of warfare on such a scale. And of course the War did not settle anything. It merely confirmed the significance of Lincoln's remark to the people of the South – "There are more of us than there are of you." Under such circumstances, violence might be expected.

Then there is the matter of the larger context. Given the insistence of many commentators on the Europeanism of this strand of the culture, I suppose it is inevitable that comparisons with Europe itself would seem irrelevant. But settlement in America coincided with a long series of catastrophic wars in Europe, which took tens of millions of lives, and which contributed mightily to our population. In 1871, when the West was wild, the French government besieged, starved, bombarbed, and defeated the city of Paris, with vast loss of life. One must ask, wild compared to what? Grief, waste, shame – history. Americans act as though they should have been immune to these things. They also act as if they invented them.

My point is simply that what happened here need not at all be attributed to conditions special to this place. It seems racist to me to say that the conflict between settlers and indigenous people on this continent had particular virulence or inevitability because it occurred between what we call races. One need only look at what Englishmen did to Englishmen in Australia, or what Frenchmen did to Frenchmen in the Vendée. Many of the Scots who came here were driven off their tribal lands by Scots landowners. Many who did not find their way here died of poverty and illness. Surely no one would question the rightness of accepting Jefferson's poor fugitives. Yet it made us a population fiercely marked by history, in our various ways. How violent might such a people be, given the human tendency to do as one is done by? Is American violence *American* violence, or something we have brought with us, as an aspect of the kinds of experience that have brought us here? By the standards of the nineteenth century, America was not particularly violent. Of course the history of the nineteenth century reads like a psychotic nightmare. I share the opinion that we have become comparatively violent in this century, though to make such a judgment, one is dependent on statistics and definitions. Hitler's and Stalin's governments reported low rates of crime. Criminal regimes usually do.

To cast the tendency toward violence back in time is to make it, once again, a part of our myth of origins. Because we were violent in that past, we are and will be violent. We are predisposed that way as, say, the French and the British are not. But if they were up to appalling things then, too, how have they escaped this predisposition? Either they have not escaped it, in which case we are not especially violent, or the nineteenth century has nothing inevitable to do with what happens in the present. If that is true, our violence has another origin, and we should look for it, rather than blaming cowboys. It is so characteristic of us to exercise our capacity for dudgeon, in the very course of evading responsibility.

Consider the classic moment of Western mythic violence, the showdown. This was reenacted obsessively in the fifties and sixties, as I recall, in films and television. It is hard now to remember what an austere ritual it was: two men approached each other from opposite ends of an empty street, stopped at a good distance from each other, and held their hands out from their holsters. The point was to determine who was "fastest." The hero had to be very fast, because the ethics of the situation forbade him to reach for his gun until his adversary reached for his. The hero was always successful. There was always something melancholy in his success because he was not at heart a violent man, or because he had wearied of violence but could not escape it. The adversary might be an old friend, or someone in whom he saw his own youth.

What historical basis any of this could have had, I cannot imagine. Any custom generally similar to it would, it seems to me, have been about as lethal as a game of catch. To pull a heavy old revolver out of a leather holster and fire it without taking time to aim – this seems to me an unlikely way to go about killing anyone. Compare European dueling, in which the pistol was carried in the hand, the combatants stood at fairly close range, and a signal was given to fire.

No doubt the showdown was a rarefied version of any number of real and imagined events involving guns and grudges and mayhem, or its near occasion. The very abstract form it took is particularly interesting because it would not have reflected innocence. Whether its origins were in the period after the Civil War or in the period after World War II and during Korea, the decades represented in the films and the decades that embraced the experience of the audience were certainly the two periods in American history when the population had been most broadly and deeply affected by violence. It is interesting that convention refined the showdown into a ritualized moment that made violence so small a part of it. By comparison, in the Eastwood period, violence became the whole of the event. While the old hero could not use his weapon until it became an act of self-defense, the new hero – I think it is coy to call him an antihero – deals death qualmlessly, businesslike as a pyrotechnician brought in for the Fourth of July.

The old showdown Westerns resembled revenge tragedy, the Elizabethan and Jacobean form in which rage or honor drove the hero to carry out a murder, at the extreme peril of his soul. I speculate that the conflict there was between chivalric culture – in which the nobility were a law unto themselves – and centralized national culture. In the sixteenth and seventeenth centuries, and again on the Western frontier, the prestige and influence of civilization and religion must have seemed about to become altogether ascendant, to supersede old codes and to disallow kinds of courage and skill they had celebrated. But the Renaissance plays are about the nightmare aspects of violence, full of bafflement, duplicity, and dread. The Western showdown was, by comparison, a rather frank, sunlit affair, a discrete act that did not litter the stage with corpses, or ruin the innocent and the guilty together. It was myth, clearly, having to do instead, I think, with the legitimation of social order. Again in the background of the myth is the recent experience of catastrophic war. The skills and virtues celebrated in wartime are intolerable in times of peace. Perhaps the myth of the pacification of the frontier rehearsed the emotional and psychological readjustment of the population to the norms of peace.

Western heroes mediated between the ungovernable souls beyond the frontier and the flow of civilization crossing the continent. Civilization was dull or corrupt or cowardly or pretentious, but it was inevitable. The hero identified with it for his own reasons, but for deep and obvious reasons, having to do with personal style, he belonged with the outlaws. In the myth, every concession is made to the way of life being suppressed. Romantic lawlessness is honorably met and defeated on its own ground. Westerns are always elegiac. Their world is always bringing itself to an end. It is not hard to imagine that the culture transacted a good deal of important business in its obsessive return to this imagined moment. Then the moment vanished.

The one thing true about any myth is that among those who are its host population it has the status of belief – not consciously held opinion, but settled assumption, with a penumbra of related assumption spreading away on every side. There is nothing harder than to know what it is we assume. I think as a culture we have ceased to encode our myths in narrative as that word is traditionally understood. Now they shield themselves from our skepticism by taking on the appearance of scientific or political or economic discourse, and they flourish, neither shaped by the expectation that they should be large and resonant and astonishing, nor self-limited as traditional myths have been because they invoke the very silences they break. What are we? Why are we here? What is being asked of us? A central myth of ours, if it were rendered as narrative, would sound like this: One is born and in passage through childhood suffers some grave harm. Subsequent good fortune is meaningless because of this injury, while subsequent misfortune is highly significant as the consequence of this injury. The work of one's life is to discover and name the harm one has suffered.

New myths do arise, and they have consequences. Cultures change. The way of thinking I describe above is essentially new but recognizably ours, and it carries us farther yet from all other cultures we admire, perhaps from all other cultures. It is a sort of latter-day, bungled Freudianism with the idea of sublimation stripped away (an implied demand, a compensation, a distraction), and the link broken between the pain of life, and adulthood, and civilization. It is a myth that allows us to keep ourselves before our eyes as the first claimant, in extreme cases the only claimant, upon our pity and indulgence. This entails indifference to certain values celebrated in older myth, for example, dignity, self-possession, magnanimity, compassion, loyalty, humor, courage, selflessness, reverence expressed as gratitude for one's experience of the goodness of life, reverence expressed as awe in face of the pain and mystery of life.

I suppose it is obvious that I consider this a mean little myth, far worse than most it presumes to displace. Try to imagine it translated into statuary or painted on temple walls, or illuminating its texts. Again, it is a myth of origins that establishes the human personality as small and victimized, fixed in childhood unless – and here is the paradox, I suppose – one recovers one's childhood. In this world of sorrow, this world we make, in which every index of grief among the young shows a dramatic upward curve, we ourselves are the children with whom we are compassionate. Once again, valuable energies are misappropriated.

The Freudian father was overthrown in order to be internalized, and the process created the adult personality. Our myth disqualifies literal and virtual parents, not only by assuming that they in essential ways have failed, but also by dismissing them as appropriate models of adulthood. It devalues adulthood as an attainment, as a work of character or imagination, and makes it merely conditional upon the circumstances of childhood.

I think there is probably a sort of fractal relation between the effect of the myth in terms of the individual and the fact of the urge to displace myth in the larger culture. We don't want to have parents, and we don't want to be parents. We reject the socializing effect of shared narratives as delusion and imposition. I am probably too aware that the past is fearsome, profoundly unsavory. But look at the world *we* make. It has never ceased to be true that the great human problem is to deal with the terrible side of human nature. We must certainly look at history with any compassion it deserves, in the hope that history will find some way to forgive us. Assuming, of course, that we allow it time and leisure to remember us.

According to one old story, God wrote, in stone, honor your mother. Think what a mother would likely have been in those days, a child herself, a minor wife or a concubine, a little straggler with nothing to show for herself but her babies. But God demanded honor for her, in the same terse code that he demanded it for Himself. Not on condition of, or in the measure of, any kind of deserving. Honor her. This commandment must have required great exertions of compassion and imagination in multitudes of cases. It must have compelled the discovery of much oblique and difficult value where, without it, only fault would have been found.

Two things are true. Everyone deserves profound respect, and no one deserves it. To understand the claim anyone has on our respect requires compassion and imagination, attentiveness and discipline. And this brings me back to the subject of the West, and its myth, and its silence.

From my memory and my experience, I conclude that the true, abiding myth of the West is that there is an intense, continuous, and typically wordless conversation between attentive people and the landscape they inhabit, and that this can be the major business of a very rich life. I suspect that Western individualism is created by the assumption that anyone may be engaged in this conversation, and therefore he or she should be treated with a certain tact and respect. This contemplative aspect of Western life is recognizably a descendant of what we misname transcendentalism, the moral/philosophic/esthetic enthusiasm that flourished in the period that established the West as a presence in the national imagination, and that otherwise expressed itself in Utopianism and Abolitionism, poetry, philosophy, and otherwise. In the West as nowhere else I have felt I was among people who appreciated, in the esthetic sense, moment by moment, altogether and in detail, the place where they were. I have noticed how patient, and generous, they were with silence. I think it is a silence Thoreau would recognize, one that retains his own inflection. This is not something the larger culture is much inclined to value. To claim so much spiritual space, to have so little impulse to allow others access to it, these are now read as signs of pathology. With all the talk there is of tolerating a variety of cultures, it is inevitable that those characterized by disfavored traits, like reserve and stoicism, should be subjected to moral disapprobation. As if the larger culture had entirely resolved the question of the proper conduct of life.

Whenever I am asked to talk about the West, my first impulse is always to express deep gratitude, and my second impulse is to express it again, because it has preserved this spacious quiet, like a secret told to me, which I keep because I cannot find words to tell it. I cannot imagine my life without it. What if, at its core, beneath all that the world can perceive or impose, the essence of Western life is ascetic and contemplative? What if our mingled lives have produced here a habit of meditation on the immanent and the actual, like nothing else, so unself-regarding that it need not promise any reward, neither enlightenment nor refinement nor prosperity nor peace nor health nor salvation? And what if we cast it off as a provincialism, or betray it to the impulse to interpret only in terms that vulgarize and devalue – our most reliable impulse in this strange time? Then, I think, the West would be gone. We would be left only with landscape.

ABOUT THE AUTHORS

AGHA SHAHID ALI is an author, editor, and translator. His most recent books are *The Half-Inch Himalayas* (1987) and *A Nostalgist's Map of America* (1991).

MARY CLEARMAN BLEW is the author of two collections of short stories, *Lambing Out* and *Runaway;* and the coeditor of *The Last Best Place: A Montana Anthology*. Her memoir, *All but the Waltz: Essays on a Montana Family*, was published in 1991.

BILL BRASHLER is the author of four novels, including *The Bingo Long Traveling All Stars and Motor Kings* (1973), *The Chosen Prey* (1982) and *Traders* (1991). He has also written a number of nonfiction books, including *Josh Gibson: A Life in the Negro Leagues* (1978) and *Catch You Later* (with Johnny Bench, 1979).

MICHAEL DENNIS BROWNE is the author of several volumes of poetry, the most recent of which are *You Won't Remember This* (1992) and *Smoke from the Fires* (1985). He is the director of creative writing at the University of Minnesota.

SIDNEY BURRIS is a professor at the University of Arkansas, and the author of *The Poetry of Resistance: Seamus Heaney and the Pastoral Tradition*.

JULIAN GLOAG was born in England, worked for many years in publishing in New York, and is the author of ten novels. His new novel, *Ultimate Help*, will be published in 1993.

MIROSLAV HOLUB was born and lives in the former Czechoslovakia, where he is a noted essayist, poet, and immunologist. His most recent literary books are *Poems Before and After* (1990) and *Dimensions of the Present Moment* (essays, 1990).

JAMES D. HOUSTON is the author of six novels, including *Gig, Love Life,* and *Continental Drift*. Among his nonfiction works is *Californians: Searching for the Golden State*, which received an American Book Award from the Before Columbus Foundation. He is currently a visiting professor in literature at the University of California, Santa Cruz.

DONALD JUSTICE is the author of many books of poetry, most recently his *Selected Poems*, for which he received the Pulitzer Prize for Poetry. He is a professor of creative writing at the University of Florida, Gainesville.

WILLIAM KITTREDGE'S most recent book is a memoir, *The Hole in the Sky* (1992). He is also the author of *Owning It All* (essays) and *We are Not in This Together* (stories). He teaches at the University of Montana.

CHRISTOPHER MERRILL is a poet, editor, and has been a director of the Santa Fe Writers' Conference. He lives in Portland, Oregon. His books of poetry are *Workbook* (1988) and *Fevers & Tides* (1989). His newest book is *From the Faraway Nearby: Georgia O'Keefe as Icon* (1992).

MARILYNNE ROBINSON is the author of *Housekeeping* (novel, 1980) and *Mother Country* (nonfiction, 1989).

JANE SMILEY'S most recent books are *Ordinary Love and Good Will* (novellas, 1989) and *A Thousand Acres*, which won the 1991 Pulitzer Prize for Fiction.

GARY SNYDER'S most recent collection of essays is *The Practice of the Wild* (1990); his *No Nature: New and Selected Poems* was released in 1992. He received the Pulitzer Prize for Poetry for *Turtle Island* (1975).